Cleeves Family

JOHN MICHAEL CLEEVES = JOAN
b 1716
d 24 Nov 1775
North Perrott

PH = (2) WILLIAM | SUSAN | = Rev. EDGAR | SIMON | = ANN | EDMUND | WILLIAM | JOAN | SARAH
) GRAY | b 1746 | | b 1748 | b 1744 | b ? |
| North Perrott | | North Perrott | | North Perrott |
771 | d 1841 | | d 23 Jul 1810 | d 1828 | d 1790 |
d 1813 | | | North Perrott | | North Perrott |

= ANN | JOSEPH | ANN
WILLY | b 1771 | b 1774
b 1780 | | East Lambrook
2 Jun 1803 |
Kingsbury Episcopl |
d 1 Feb 1839 |
North Perrott |

RINE | JANE
3 | b 8 Feb 1824
eth | Thornfalcon
01 | d 1900

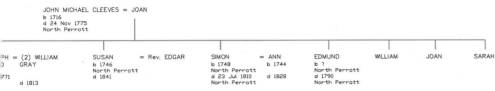

THE OLD BREWERY, BRIDPORT

The old Brewery, Bridport which had been established in 1794, was bought in 1896 by John Cleeves Palmer and his younger brother Robert Henry. Cleeves ran the Brewery and its pubs, while Henry managed his estate at West Bexington Manor and later at Puncknowle Manor. Today the Brewery is run by his great grandsons, John & Cleeves Palmer.

ROBERT HENRY = OCTAVIA EVELYN
b 11 Aug 1867 | ALDRIDGE FLOWER
West Bexington | b 1870
| m – 4 Apr 1899
d 26 Mar 1933 | d 7 Apr 1955
Puncknowle | Shipton

GRACE AUGUSTA | EVELINE JANE ELIZABETH = WALTER HERMANN | EMMELINE MARY FLOWER = WILLIAM ARTHUR
FLOWER BARTLETT | b 2 Apr 1900 | AMSTUTZ | (MOLLY) | MUDD
b 23 Jan 1892 | West Bexington | b 5 Dec 1902 | b 27 Jun 1903 | b 28 May 1882
West Knighton | | Brienzwiler, Switzerland | West Bexington | m – 25 Apr 1934
– 27 Dec 1915 Bombay, India | d 28 Oct 1993 | m – 25 Apr 1930 | d 25 Mar 1993 | d 27 Mar 1953
d 11 Jul 1981 | Mannedorf, Switzerland | Pucknowle | Pingelly, Australia
Winterbourne Steepleton | | d 6 Aug 1997
| | Mannedorf, Switzerland

FLOWER = (1) ARTHUR ANTHONY JOHN = (2) ALBAN EDWARD
| | COURTENAY WYLDE
| b 4 Feb 1918, Southwold | b 6 Sep 1918, London
| m – 2 Mar 1946 | m – 10 Jun 1989
| Reigate | Bridport
| d 19 Mar 1986 |
| Bridport |

ROSEMARY | KATHERINE | ANTHONY JOHN CLEEVES = LUCILLE TONIA | CLEEVES WILLIAM ROBERT = EDWINA THERESE
b 7 Oct 1949, Bridport | b 7 Oct 1949, Bridport | b 26 Sep 1951 | JARROLD | b 14 Aug 1962 | de CANDAMO
d 8 Oct 1949, Bridport | d 7 Oct 1949, Bridport | Bridport | b 12 Apr 1963 Norwich | Bridport | b 4 Nov 1964 Bishop's Stortford
| | | m – 29 Apr 1989 Norwich | | m – 10 Dec 1994 Bere Regis

ANTHONY CHARLES = JULIA ELIZABETH | QUINTIN ROBERT | EMILY GRACE | ROSALIE KATHERINE | ALEXA FLORENCE | KITTY ELANOR | SOPHIE EMMA | MARK CLEEVES ANTHONY
| GIBBINS | b 5 Jan 1979 | b 30 Jan 1991 | b 4 Jul 1994 | b 6 Aug 1998 | b 21 Jun 2001 | b 17 May 1996 | b 2 Nov 1998
| b 28 Jun 1977 | Bushley | Dorchester | Dorchester | Dorchester | Dorchester | Dorchester | Dorchester
| High Wycombe | | | | | | |
| m – 21 Jun 2003 Great Hamden | | | | | | |

ELLEN MARY
b 19 Mar 2007
Aylesbury

PALMERS

The Story of a Dorset Brewer

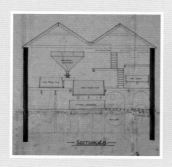

PALMERS

The Story of a Dorset Brewer

BREWERY
OFFICE
· • ·
ESTABLISHED 1794

Tim Heald

Research by Richard Sims

First published in Great Britain in 2008
by Palmers Brewery, The Old Brewery, West
Bay Road, Bridport, Dorset DT6 4JA

www.palmersbrewery.com

Text by Tim Heald

ISBN: 978-0-956 1025-0-8

A CIP catalogue record for this book is
available from the British Library

Printed and bound in Great Britain
by Butler Tanner & Dennis, Frome

10 9 8 7 6 5 4 3 2 1

Produced for Palmers Brewery
by Flanders Publishing

Project Editor Julian Flanders

Designer Carole Melbourne

Production Nick Heal

All photographs and memorabilia have been
taken from the Palmers Brewery archives
except the following:

Bridport Museum pages 19, 27, 36, 43, 83 and
89 (both); Corbis page 13; Dorset Publishing
Company/Rodney Legg pages 17 (left), 24, 45,
52, 54, 72, 78, 86, 88, 90, 91 and 92; Mary
Evans Picture Library pages 11, 18 and 21.

Special photography by Carole Melbourne

Contents

BAGSHOT PARK

Wessex is known for a great many things, but over the years I have come to appreciate that as a region it is especially good at producing a rich variety of food and drink. The Brewery in Bridport is just one example, but an exceedingly fine one not just for its produce, but also its tradition. They have been brewing and distributing ales and beers from here since 1794.

It may seem as if the Palmer family have always owned The Brewery but, as this book reveals, the truth is they've only been running it since 1896! Nevertheless the four generations have succeeded in keeping it going through the ups and downs and no doubt hope that future generations will do their best to keep the tradition going for many years to come.

A great deal of painstaking research has been undertaken to furnish the author with more than sufficient material to put this book together. I trust that you will find Richard Sims' and Tim Heald's efforts worthwhile and that you will discover new aspects of Wessex and Bridport's history as well as revealing much about the tradition of The Brewery.

HRH The Earl of Wessex KG KCVO

In the Beginning

This is the story of a family business in an ancient and beautiful corner of rural England. It's a story of tradition, survival and community. It's a story that defies trend, political correctness and smart metropolitan thinking. Above all it's a tale of Englishness. This is an account of local life and how it works: a true story: no spin, no gloss, no hype.

This is how it was, how it is, and, with luck, how it will be. Real life is not about headlines; it's about the day-to-day, the unsung, and what could be mistaken for the ordinary. A long-standing family business making the most English of drinks in one of the most English corners of the country is not the stuff of headlines but it is a fascinating slice of reality.

The Palmer family make beer in West Dorset. The coast in this part of the country, known as the 'Jurassic Coast', was one of England's first Natural World Heritage Sites and is a breathtaking seascape with towering fossil-filled cliffs. But the land behind it is also magnificent in an unchanging English way, immortalised in the stories of the greatest of all Dorset novelists, Thomas Hardy.

Opposite Magnificent in an unchanging English way – the cliffs at West Bay, Bridport.

People have been making beer and drinking it here for centuries though they
have been doing it elsewhere for even longer. Barley, the main raw ingredient in
the making of beer, existed as far back as 3000 BC. Neolithic man grew it in his
valleys and ancient hieroglyphs suggest that the Egyptians made some sort of
alcoholic beverage from barley, though no one really knows if it tasted anything
like good old English bitter.

The Anglo-Saxons called the drink 'ealu' which
probably derived from the Scandinavian 'ol' and the
Lithuanian 'alus'. 'Beer', which was the Anglo-Saxon
'beor', came from German 'bier' and Icelandic 'bjorr'.
It could have been the Anglo-Saxons who first
brought the drink with them when they invaded our
shores or it might have been the Romans. Tacitus
mentions a barley-based beverage and so does

Herodotus. The Romans indeed could be credited with inventing the pub though
the original Roman taverns would have sold wine rather than beer. The Romans
certainly invented the inn sign which in those days was always a garland or bush
of evergreens – it's because of this that we still have pubs called by such names as
the Old Bull and Bush. It's not, however, beyond the bounds of possibility that the
ancient Britons and Celts concocted something along similar lines before any
foreigners first arrived. In truth no one really knows.

What is definitely true is that brewing beer and drinking it is something that
English people have done for hundreds of years, probably about 2000 years but maybe
more. In the Middle Ages beer was the most common of all British drinks and the
original Full English Breakfast would have meant a chine of beef, a loaf of bread and a
gallon of ale. Until the early fifteenth century ale would have consisted simply of
malted barley, water and yeast. The resulting liquid would have been opaque and
cloudy but highly nutritious and bursting with proteins and carbohydrates.

The Normans, who were keen on order and organisation unlike the more
anarchic natives, were the first rulers of Britain to give brewing a basic structure.
Establishing a network of abbeys and monasteries throughout the land, they added
on breweries and alehouses for the refreshment of the monks and the travellers
who were entertained by them. By the time of Henry IV, 300 years after the
Conquest, there was a national guild of brewers and as time passed so brewing and

beer became a source of income for the Exchequer under the authority and control of the Crown.

In West Dorset the production and consumption of beer has historically followed the same pattern as in other parts of England, though the local evidence is often sketchy. The Bridport town records for 1267, the earliest to survive, show that the price for which ale could be sold was related directly to the price of barley.

Opposite A modern sign for the Old Bull and Bush, which reflects the pub name's Roman heritage.

Above The Full English Breakfast in medieval times would have included roast beef and bread washed down with beer.

If, for example, the market price of barley was four shillings per quarter then the ale was to be sold at a penny per four quarts; at three shillings per quarter the ale was to be sold at four pence per four quarts. The penalty for breaking this rule on more than one occasion was to be carried around the town in a tumbrel, a cart often used to take prisoners to their execution and famously described by Charles Dickens in his novel *A Tale of Two Cities* hundreds of years later.

It was quite usual, in those early days, for landlords to sell beer by the jar or mug irrespective of how much liquid these receptacles contained. In 1349, however, two people in West Dorset were fined three pence each for selling ale in jars of different sizes. People who did this were brought before the Assize of Ale, and in 1473 more than 60 people were fined between tuppence and four pence for various similar misdemeanours to do with beer. In 1529 and again in 1556 more fines were levied against brewers who had not conformed to legal standards in their beers. Although legislation regarding beer remained patchy by the 1500s the authorities obviously wanted to regulate the trade.

In Chaucer's time Britain's first hops were imported by merchants from Holland and Flanders. Hops acted as a preservative and they also imparted bitterness and aroma to the ale. For years the 'hopped' drink was called 'beer' and the 'un-hopped' beverage 'ale'. But by the eighteenth century 'un-hopped' drinks had died out and strictly speaking, there was no longer such a thing as ale.

By then alehouses, as they were usually and perhaps perversely known, were licensed. In 1593 a Bridport landlord called Alexander Primrose had to guarantee to the authorities that he would sell 'wholesome' ale, beer, bread and other victuals and allow no unlawful games to take place. In addition he had to keep one bed available for the subjects of Elizabeth I, and was not to refuse anyone sent by the bailiffs.

At this time many publicans would have been brewing and selling their own ale and beer on their own premises. This would usually be standard stuff but at certain times of the year special celebratory ales were produced. In Bridport these included Church, Whitsun, Lamb, Clerk, Bride and Robin Hood Ales. We know that in 1555 Robin Hood Ale was being brewed by Henry Waye and Stephen Shower. The ingredients were collected from the townspeople and the beer was sold on the festival day of Robin Hood. The profits generated were used to repair the local roads and bridges.

In 1594 a new by-law was passed requiring the owners of tippling houses to set out an ale stake or pole to advertise the fact that they sold ale or beer. In return they were allowed to keep one gallon of the beer for their own use and the rest could be sold for use on or off the premises.

Up to the seventeenth century, while Bridport's licensed victuallers and owners of tippling houses brewed the beer and ale for sale, home brewing accounted for the majority of the beer and ale actually consumed. Like cider making in this apple-growing part of the world, brewing was essentially a cottage industry.

The Brewing Process

Monks were among the earliest brewers in Europe.

The beer brewing process in the sixteenth century was less sophisticated than it is today but the principles were the same or similar. From beginning to end there were six stages: grinding, mashing, boiling, cooling, fermenting and racking. After it had been cleaned and crushed or 'ground' the barley or 'grist' was mixed or 'mashed' with hot liquor in a 'mash tun' which stood for a while to complete the 'mashing'. The liquid, then called 'wort', was transferred into a copper and boiled up with hops. Once it had become 'hopped wort' it was cooled and dropped into fermenting vessels and mixed with yeast. Finally, after seven days, the liquid was run into casks for the final 'racking'. It was then, more or less, beer. Time and technology, as well as changing taste and increased knowledge, have led to important and significant changes but basically brewing is as simple as that – though as any Palmer will tell you, it is actually a great deal more complicated.

In a town like Bridport whose roofs were largely thatched until the late eighteenth century the fires required in the brewing process often ran out of control. In 1614 to counter this threat the town council bought in a regulation at the County Sessions, which required licensed victuallers and common tippling houses to take their beer from the town brewhouse. Although that too was a thatched building, the fire risk was perceived as lower as the beer was being brewed in one place rather than in hundreds of unsupervised and highly combustible cottages. Of course, it also led to a much greater consistency in the quality of the local beer and made the whole business much easier to control and regulate.

The Bridport Town Brewhouse and Malthouse, a low, L-shaped building between West Mill and the Gundry's Court building, was almost certainly in operation by 1614 though that didn't prevent illegal brewing elsewhere. This important local landmark not only brewed the town's beer but also malted the town's barley for itself and for the home brewers who still accounted for most of the beer produced in the town's private homes. An inventory of 1650 shows that the brewhouse was well-equipped with a furnace pan (copper), four 'cool backers' or coolers and three great vats or brewing vessels. There was also a horse-operated mill for grinding the malt.

The brewhouse remained in private hands until 1650 when the town council purchased it from Thomas Bartlett and his son Francis, with a bequest made by Jane Napier of Puncknowle (pronounced 'Punnel'), a picturesque neighbouring village. The condition of this bequest was that the profits from the brewhouse were to be used for the relief of the poor and needy of Bridport. These poor children were to be apprenticed to artificers or tradesmen, while their poor parents were given money to buy materials for 'their professions to labour upon'. It sounds a touch paternalistic but it did establish the idea that local brewing should have a philanthropic as well as a profitable dimension.

The brewhouse was initially leased out for seven years at a time but by 1723 the length of the leases increased markedly when Samuel Symes took over.

Opposite The Hyde, family seat of the Gundrys – bankers, manufacturers of textiles, rope makers, net makers and, above all, brewers and the first owners of the Old Brewery in Bridport.

Significant names now began to appear in the history of Bridport brewing for Symes' partner was probably Samuel Gundry, and the two of them certainly bought another brewery from someone called Mordecai Legg that same year.

After almost 20 years, in 1742, another Gundry, John – described as a 'maltster' – took over the lease with Robert Bull, a mercer, and William Davie, who was categorised simply as 'gent'. This time the lease was for 99 years. John Gundry died in 1763, but William Davie carried on the business, possibly with other partners, including John's nephew Samuel, until the end of 1771. In 1773 another Gundry – Joseph – seems to have run the brewhouse until it reverted to the 'cofferers', or town treasurers, in 1778.

The Gundrys, however, continued to make beer, though no longer at the town brewhouse. In 1793, Samuel Gundry VI took over the family's modest textile and beer-brewing business on the death of his father Samuel V. He was happy enough with the way things were going in textiles but he had more ambitious plans for the brewing side of the business. In March 1794 he and a partner purchased a meadow called Fives Yard on the outskirts of Bridport and it was here that the Old Brewery was built, it remains on the same site to this day.

Luckily for Samuel Gundry VI the family textile business benefited from the Napoleonic Wars: sailcloth, webs, ropes and netting were all purchased by the Royal Navy. The profits from these activities paid for the building of the brewery and the brewing of the beer. There was a pleasing symmetry to this: Gundry paid his textile workers for their labours and they in turn paid him for his beer. So, in a sense, the money just went round and round.

The construction of the new building took the best part of two years and was an elaborate project for a quiet and not particularly prosperous corner of England. It probably opened in the autumn of 1796. More than two centuries later its layout is relatively unchanged. The original brewhouse itself was on the corner of Eype Road and the River Brit. To the south was the malthouse and to the east was the fermenting room. Below this was the cellar for racking the beer and alongside this was another cellar for ale storage. Stables, a carpenter's shop and cask cleaning area completed the site. When it was finished in 1796 the brewery was at the cutting edge of brewing technology – a model of its kind.

The expensive and sophisticated building suggested that not only was Gundry beer good enough to be drunk throughout the region but that if the war went well

The Brewery's Earliest Pubs

The Greyhound (above) and the George Inn (right) – two of the brewery's earliest purchases.

An important step for any self-respecting brewery was to build up an empire of local pubs through which to sell its beer. Bridport had its fair share of pubs, many of which were opened to take advantage of the popularity of the town's market, which had developed since it first began in the fifteenth century. The first acquisition was the lease of the Sloop at Bridport Harbour (now West Bay) in 1798. The Sloop was then the only pub at the harbour. A year later Gundry bought a half share in the Royal Oak in Bridport and in 1801 he added the lease of the Greyhound, an important coaching inn on the town's main street. In 1802 he bought the freehold of the George Inn at the top of South Street and the

lease of the New Inn in West Street. Finally, he took a lease on the White Bull on East Road. Within seven years of its opening the new brewery therefore had an impressive little cluster of Bridport pubs in its empire.

Rather like a successful Monopoly player Gundry now decided that it was time to consolidate. He didn't buy another Bridport property for five years. Instead he turned his attentions the surrounding countryside. In 1800 he failed in attempts to buy pubs in Chideock and Lyme Regis but succeeded in buying his first country property when he acquired the lease of the White Lion at Broadwindsor a few miles north of Bridport three years later.

and Britain won control of the seas then there might be a market for it abroad. Unlike his ancestors Samuel Gundry VI had far-reaching ambitions.

The Napoleonic Wars were good for beer as well as textiles. The British fleet used Torbay as a harbour during hostilities and in the brewing season from October 1799 to June 1800 over 1000 barrels of Gundry porter, worth over £1800 was shipped to the fleet from Bridport harbour, usually on board the *Sylph* or the *Mercury*. In March 1802, however, Britain and France signed the Treaty of Amiens and the fleet moved on, taking the sailors' thirst with it. It was not the last time that war had a massive but short-lived impact on Bridport brewing.

The loss of this lucrative naval trade was a blow. To offset it Gundry and Company wrote to their contacts in Devon touting for trade, offering beer at 54 shillings and porter for 44 shillings per barrel. But the Devon men took no porter and little stout. Simultaneous attempts to set up a Plymouth base were also only partly successful although there was a regular shipping link between the two places and some of the vessels were part-owned by Gundry. At the same time a steady and regular trade with London for the stout beer produced in Bridport was established but the amounts were always small.

Meanwhile Gundry took over part control of a local mill and became a partner in the Bridport Bank. This, inevitably, meant he had less time for the brewery and in 1816 he transferred his half share in its freehold to his son, Samuel Bowden Gundry. His was a brewery with modern plant of the latest design, put together with an eye on efficiency. Yet finding a viable market remained a problem and it even seems likely that every year, in common with rival breweries, Gundry's brewing may have ceased altogether from June to October, so that there was no production of beer for more than a third of the entire year. Such seasonality could never be cost-effective.

After the end of the Napoleonic Wars the Gundry Company continued to expand. It purchased more pubs in Bridport and these gave it control of most of the important licensed houses in East and West Streets. They ran along the Great West Road, which was the main thoroughfare for travellers passing through town. After 1820, however, there were no further acquisitions for six years, when the Anchor at Burton Bradstock was taken on a long lease from the Pitt Rivers estate. This was

Opposite The British fleet at anchor off Torbay in 1799.

Above A £1 note issued in 1807 by the Bridport Bank and signed by Joseph Gundry.

followed by the purchase of two houses in North Allington, the Boot and the Kings Arms in 1826 and two final acquisitions in 1828: the Swan at Burton Bradstock and the Mail Coach Inn at Charmouth, which later changed its name to the Coach and Horses. The company also acquired a long lease on the White Lion at West Bridge. By now the company owned 23 houses, of which 13 were freehold.

Private trade was a small part of the business and was given up when the expansion caused by the 1830 Beer Act took hold. Basically this legislation was designed to mitigate the effects of excessive gin drinking. 'Drunk for a penny, dead drunk for tuppence' was the gin-drinker's maxim and beer was widely considered to be an acceptably innocent alternative. Everyone drank it – even children took 'small beer'. The 1830 Act made it possible for any citizen who paid out two guineas to turn his home into a beer shop, licensed for the sale of beer and cider but not spirits. These places were known as 'Tom and Jerry Houses'. This term derives its name from Corinthian Tom and Jerry Hawthorn Esq, the two chief characters in a popular novel of the time called *Life in London* by Pierce Egan, which was published in 1821. These two young men about town gave a lively account of the city's sporting gallants and amusements in the days of the Regency when riotous behaviour (to 'tom and jerry'), brought about by too much beer, started on Thursday and went on until Sunday night. It doesn't take much to realise why the famous cartoon series took the same name.

After the Act, overall output of Gundry's beer increased to around 6000 barrels per year, doubling in two years from the previous average level. The Act also led to a doubling of the number of licensed houses in Bridport, which included the Sailor's Home in South Street. Many of the new beer houses were little more than a room in an ordinary house, but they gave South Street a reputation as a street where every other house was a pub. It looks as if the Gundry Company supplied an additional 30 houses over a two-year period after the Act came into force. Most of the new customers would have been Tom and Jerry Houses, few of which brewed their own beer, at least in the Bridport area. They were simply cashing in on the 1830 Act and when the government, alarmed by the massive expansion in beer drinking they had triggered, reined in the new houses with much tighter rules, many of the new landlords went out of business.

By the 1830s brewing was being carried out the whole year round. In winter, when most of the stronger beers were produced, brewing usually took place twice

a week. In summer this dropped to once a week. By 1832 the brewery was reaching capacity. Few improvements had been made since its opening; Samuel Gundry had concentrated more and more on his banking business and eventually, aged 66, bowed out altogether.

Above Corinthian Tom and Jerry Hawthorne make free with the drinks in this illustration by George Cruikshank, 1824.

Great Reforms

In 1832, the year of the Great Reform Act, a new partnership of four headed by Gundry's son, Samuel Bowden Gundry, took over the running of the Bridport brewery. As if to emphasise the importance of the local beer the town celebrated the passing of the Act on 8 August with a procession and a celebratory dinner at which 80 casks of a special brewery-brewed ale were drunk. Here, as elsewhere, there was a traditional link between beer and politics.

The Act introduced huge changes to the electoral system in England and Wales. The previous system, one that had prevailed since before the Civil War of 1642, had seen Dorset send 20 Members to Parliament. At the passing of the Act there were only 1225 people in the whole of Dorset qualified to vote – an average of 61 electors per MP – though this was by no means the worst record in the country. Rural areas with such numerical representation in Parliament had become known as 'rotten boroughs' and stood in stark contrast to the large urban areas that had grown as a result of the Industrial Revolution.

Opposite The beer brewing process has changed little over the years. These men, working at the Old Brewery in the nineteenth century, are carrying similar tools to those used at the brewery today.

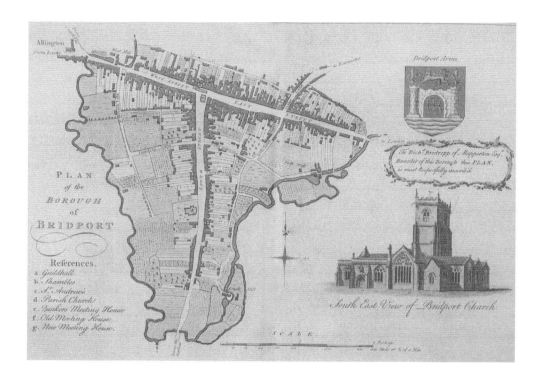

As a result of the Act, Dorset sent three Members to Parliament and the number of people eligible to vote increased dramatically. The Act was greeted with joy as it meant that there were more voters. In reality, it also meant there were more people to bribe.

Beer, always a feature of political life in West Dorset, really did play an important and controversial part in a hotly contested election a few years later. In 1846 the sitting member, a Tory called Alexander Baillie-Cochrane, was elected by a single vote over the Whig John Romilly. Parliament smelt a rat and a Select Committee was appointed to investigate whether bribery had been involved. After much deliberation they decided that it had and overturned the result. The committee found that a cordwainer named Rockett had taken several drinks in the George, which was a well-known Cochrane house, and also took money from Mr Cochrane's servant. He had at least one drink in the King of Prussia and

Above A map of the 'rotten borough' of Bridport in 1795.

another in the Pack Horse. The investigation turned on a memorable discussion between the committee and Rockett. This included the exchange, 'Had you any drink then?' To which Rockett replied, 'I cannot say now; I had drunk a trifle, but nothing to take away any of my faculties.' Whether or not he was drinking a beer brewed by the Gundry partnership is not recorded.

The new brewery quartet consisted of Samuel Bowden Gundry, John Gundry Downe, William Battiscombe and James Templer. Samuel Bowden Gundry retained ownership of the freehold of the brewery and leased it to the partnership. All the other property was divided among the new partners, though the divisions were neither equal nor straightforward. For example, Samuel Bowden Gundry personally held on to the freehold of the Boot at Allington and Elizabeth Rooker (née Gundry) held the late Samuel Symes' shares in the brewery freehold and also in the Royal Oak.

Samuel Bowden Gundry had been involved with the brewery since 1816 when he was given his father's share in the freehold. He had married and moved to Loders Court in the country nearby before later returning to Bridport where he lived in the late Daniel Gundry's house in West Street. Unlike his father, Samuel Bowden Gundry seems to have concentrated on the brewery business and had nothing to do with textiles or banking.

The Downe family into which he married had been an important link in the business. They ran Downe's Wharf in London and John Gundry Downe, another of the four partners, was Samuel Bowden Gundry's wife's uncle. He had been a partner since the brewery's beginning.

William Battiscombe was an accountant. His family had been involved in the licensed trade since his grandfather had taken over the Sun in West Street, next door to Samuel Gundry V's house. The family was also involved in the Sailor's Home and the Five Bells, both in South Street. The brewery had been supplying these houses since the 1830s and William's stepmother, Elizabeth, was the sister of John Rose one of the original partners of the business.

James Templer was born in Launceston, Cornwall, in 1787 and seems to have arrived in Bridport in the early 1820s setting up a solicitor's practice with his brother, Henry. In 1811 James married Catherine Lethbridge and one of their children, George O' Kelly Templer, was to play a significant role in the later history of the brewery.

The partnership added a few buildings to the brewery and in 1838 spring water from a field to the west of the brewery replaced the original well-water supply. The company had leased the field since 1799 and this source of water is still used today.

Some time in the 1840s they almost certainly built a new boiler house for the introduction of steam power. In the early twenty-first century the building was still there though it was no longer used as a boiler house. It would originally have fed a steam engine used to supplement the old waterwheel.

In November 1847 Samuel Gundry the elder and his son Walter Eustace Gundry were both declared bankrupt following the failure of the Bridport Bank. This was a catastrophe, which attracted national attention and is still a significant item in legal history and usage. The debts stood at an alarming £120,000. Samuel Gundry had been involved in the bank since 1810 and been sole owner since 1823. Luckily he had no direct financial involvement with the brewery but some of the brewery funds were almost certainly held by the bank. A paltry 6/8d in the £1 was paid out the following year, which also saw the death of the bankrupt Samuel, by then an old man in his 80s.

This setback was mercifully peripheral and the partnership spent the period to the 1850s slowly buying up new properties. In 1834 they bought the Five Bells in South Street. The Clarkstone family had owned this until 1776, but the current occupant was Mary Battiscombe, sister of William. In 1836 the firm took over the Horse Street Brewery in Lyme Regis, which included the George and the Angel houses in the town together with the Blue Ball at Dottery and the Anchor Inn at Seatown. To this they added in 1839, the Cross Keys in South Street and the Boot Inn in North Allington, which was bought from Samuel Gundry himself.

John Gundry Downe died in 1843 and William Battiscombe in 1849. Downe's share of the company passed to his brothers Nathaniel and Daniel. The latter died shortly after and this left Nathaniel with the full quarter share. In 1845 Nathaniel arranged with Walter Eustace Gundry to buy Daniel's share for £3440, valuing the business at £13,760, excluding the brewery. Walter Gundry put down a deposit of £1000 but in 1847 he was declared bankrupt. Because of this Samuel Bowden Gundry bought the residue of the share two years later.

The history of the other one-eighth share was even more convoluted though few of the internecine financial transactions were simple and not everyone seems to have managed their affairs as efficiently as others. Bankrupt investors were bad for business.

After the death of William Battiscombe in 1849 his executors retained his shares on behalf of his wife Elizabeth. In 1856, however, it was agreed that they should be jointly purchased by Samuel Bowden Gundry and George Templer for £5802 11s 2½d. This gave the brewery an overall value of £23,210, almost double what it had been worth two years earlier.

By September 1856, therefore, the brewery had just two partners, Samuel Bowden Gundry and George Templer. Together they directed business for the next eight years but increasingly they relied on management staff at the brewery to carry out the day-to-day work. In 1851 William Gillard was the manager and lived at the brewery house while John Downton was his brewer and lived in Fives Court Terrace, which by now had become the traditional home for the brewer.

In the 1850s there seems to have been a change in company policy. Even though the business was thriving the company stopped buying freeholds and turned to acquiring leases instead. From 1850 to 1853 nine houses were taken on with leases. Most were in or around Bridport but two were in neighbouring Lyme Regis. Ten further leaseholds were bought between 1857 and 1864. Seven of these were in the Bridport area but two were more distant: the Alexandra Tavern in Chickerell, Weymouth, and the Union Hotel, later renamed the Clown Tavern, in Bristol. The Bristol house also served as a beer store for the export and free trade. By now the brewery owned or leased nearly 40 houses.

It was the opening of the Bridport Railway in 1857 that made the more distant properties seem viable and which expanded the brewery's territorial ambitions. The new rail link allowed Gundry Downe and Company's beers to be sent longer distances but it also meant that rival beers could be sold in Bridport. With the opening of Bridport Station a number of new pubs opened for business, including

Above Joseph Gundry, chairman of the Bridport Railway Company.

the Railway Tavern, the Railway Inn and the Railway Terminus, to take advantage of the travelling public.

An inventory of the brewery for 1865 shows, in effect, a modern brewery within the old original shell. The list of contents is esoteric-sounding to a layman but impressive nonetheless. The brewhouse boasted two 'mash tuns' made of English oak. Both were fed by 'grist cases' and each 'mash tun' was fitted with a cast iron mashing machine and a two-armed revolving copper 'sparge'. These fed into a 60-barrel 'underback' made of foreign oak and supported on iron columns.

From here the 'wort' was taken to one of three coppers. The 'hop back' was made of 3-inch Dantzie timber with a cast iron false bottom. Cooling of the 'wort' was carried out by a combination of old coolers, shallow wooden tanks supported by a large refrigerator. Fermentation took two days after which the beer was cleansed in a 100-barrel 'cleansing back' made of deal, a process that lasted at least a week.

There were three 'settling backs' one underground in the brewhouse, another near the coolers and the third, of 100 barrels capacity, in Cellar No. 1 (the main cask ale cellar up until 2008). It was here and in Cellar No. 2 (the mineral water factory from 1987–2007) that the racking and storing of beer took place. The 24 vats were to be found in Cellars 3 (the beer bottling hall until 2007) and 4 (the mineral water factory until 1987).

The 'wash house' was below the brewhouse and held the liquor tanks on stone piers. Through an archway and under the large copper was a 15-horsepower egg-ended boiler complete with brick setting. This powered the 14-hp high-pressure steam engine which complemented the waterwheel, which itself generated 5hp. Both were connected to the shafting and could work the mashing machine and the three sets of 'three-throw pumps'. The boiler was also used to generate steam for the cask-washing shed, which lay to the north opposite the brewery off the lane to Eype.

Off the washhouse to the south was No. 2 Malthouse, which was part of the original structure, a three-storey building with the kiln at the north end. In 1857 a new malthouse was built to the south end of the property to cope with the increased demand for malt following the rise in beer output. This was another three-storey building with the first malting floor made of slate on a sprung wooden floor. On the road to the Fives Court entrance was another steam yard, this one had a 4-hp boiler under a lean-to shed which fed a 2-hp high-pressure

Opposite Bridport railway station, opened in 1857, took the brewery's beer to more distant customers than ever before but also meant that rival beers could be sold in the town.

Above The brewhouse as it was in the late nineteenth century.

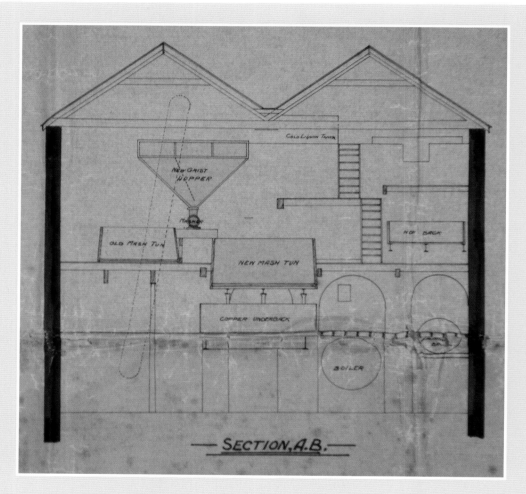

Plans, drawn up by Llewellins & James of Bristol, show the Old Brewery in the mid-19th century
as a modern, state-of-the-art plant, ready to cope with the increasing demands of its expanding
customer base.

steam engine. This was linked to a 'force pump' and 'suction main' from the river
and a rising main. The boiler also fed a steaming apparatus for 16 casks. At the
front of the brewery alongside West Bay Road, where the offices are now, were the
stables, cooper's shop and hop loft. The brewery possessed nine horses and a
mixture of drays and other wagons.

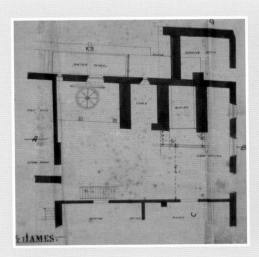

Ground Floor   First Floor

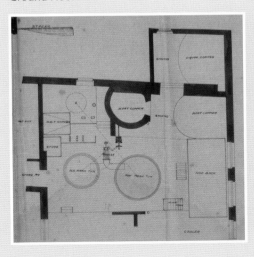

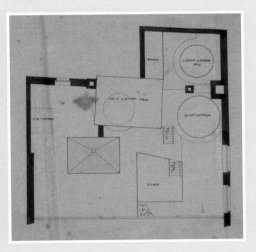

Second Floor   Third Floor

In 1861 Henry Dickenson Gundry, Samuel's son, became the manager of the brewery supervising the head brewer, Alfred Winstanley, who styled himself a 'professional' brewer. Apart from brewing beer the firm was also now bottling it. The 1861 census recorded seven beer bottlers, all young men from London who were lodging at the Fives Court and the Crown Inn.

From 1862, a year after the census, brewing books survive which give us an insight into the scale of activity as well as valuable clues about the changes which were taking place at the brewery. By 1862 no less than 12 different beers were being produced. The traditional beers were still made but in smaller quantities, with the new 'Burton' ales proving ever more popular. Meanwhile, the company's geographical horizons were expanding further and further. Their new Pale Ale was being shipped as far afield as Calcutta, Melbourne and Brisbane and in April 1863 25 hogsheads of Pale Ale were sent to Vancouver for the French Emperor Napoleon III. Throughout this period some 150 barrels of Best Bitter were brewed for Newfoundland, and sailed there annually on the same vessel that carried the nets and lines produced by the neighbouring Gundry's and Hounsell's textile firms.

In January 1863, however, Gundry Downe sold four of its houses to Thomas Legg of the rival New Brewery. This raised some £1800 pounds. The precise reason for selling them is obscure but it does cast a doubt on the performance of

Above The Fives Court Inn, which stood next door to the brewery, was home to seven young men brought down from London to do the bottling according to the 1861 census.

the business and perhaps explains at least partly why, in the summer of 1864, the Bridport Old Brewery Company Limited took over the running of the Old Brewery from Gundry Downe and Company.

Samuel Bowden Gundry, now 72 years old, had relinquished control of the running of the brewery to his son, Henry Dickenson Gundry. George Templer had apparently opted out and moved to London to work as a barrister. Templer's financial affairs were complicated and unsatisfactory and he eventually sold out to Gundry. This made it even more obvious that to compete with national breweries such as Whitbread and Bass more money had to be found and it was decided by all concerned that a new company had to be formed to run the business.

On 12 July 1864 this new company took over the brewing operation paying £13,317 for the stock in trade, with William Charlton assuming managerial control from Henry Gundry. After 70 years the Gundry family dynasty was apparently ended. On 16 July 1864 a celebration dinner was held to mark the launch of the Bridport Old Brewery Company Limited. The diners included the former brewery manager Henry Gundry, son of Samuel Bowden Gundry, William Charlton, the new manager who had masterminded the change, William Meggerson, Mrs King and Mrs Dircks, Henry Charlton, the Bristol agent, Robert Wilson, the firm's travelling clerk, John Stickland the brewery clerk, and Richard Loveless, the commercial clerk.

The change in ownership was paradoxically prompted by success and particularly the increased demand for Bridport ales in London and foreign markets. William Charlton proposed the scheme to the other eventual partners after discussing it with business associates in London. His London acquaintances told him that an extension of capital was the only way forward if they wished to be the equal of national names in places such as Burton-on-Trent.

The formal conveyance took place the following March with Samuel Bowden Gundry signing over his interest in the old company to William Charlton. Samuel Bowden Gundry was to be paid £28,125 for the business, the stock in trade having already been taken over for £13,317. Of that £25,000 was to be retained by the Bridport Old Brewery Company Limited (BOBC); £20,000 on a 5 per cent mortgage to Samuel Bowden Gundry and £5000 to pay off a loan from the Edinburgh Assurance Company Ltd. Gundry was to receive just £3125 in cash, in addition to the £158 received annually from the mortgage.

Having taken over the running of the brewery on 12 July 1864 the BOBC had to be formally registered under the 1862 Companies Act. This was done on 19 August. The seven promoters were all from the London area, and included the barrister George Templer who had so recently made over his interest in the brewery to Samuel Bowden Gundry. The others were merchants in the Barnes Company at whose Mincing Lane address the new company was initially registered.

One thousand five hundred shares of £100 were issued and George Templer agreed to take 100 as promoter. The share register for July 1865 shows 34 shareholders taking 600 of the available shares, of which 100 were apparently purchased in the name of Samuel Bowden Gundry a few days prior to the inaugural AGM. With 26 of the shareholders based in London or the suburbs and owning 70 per cent of the shares, control of the brewery was now centred more than a hundred miles from West Dorset.

Encouraged by this, the directors reported favourably to the shareholders in July 1865 and announced a profit of £4500. They then set about a new round of improvements, erecting a new brick beer store and enlarging the tied estate. Five new houses were leased in 1865, all outside Bridport itself, including the Royal Oak at Beaminster and the Fox and Star Inns at Portland.

The next year the production of several beers fell dramatically because the export market had collapsed, due apparently to circumstances beyond the brewers' control. In September 1866 Mr Price, the firm's accountant, was called in to confirm the directors' worst fears. He urged them to stop trading as soon as possible. At the subsequent shareholders' meeting James Williams was nominated to be the liquidator and the company's solicitors, Payne and Leyton, made an application for a voluntary winding-up order. Two other petitions were sent by the end of the week pressing for a compulsory winding up order and in January 1867 it was decided by the Master of the Rolls to wind the company up under the provisions of the Companies Act of 1862. This event is still looked into for 'case law', as it was one of the few occasions when an EGM has been held without all the shareholders having been informed first.

With the benefit of hindsight the collapse seems not only sudden and unexpected, but also contrary to what looks like a generally healthy situation. Business had seemed good; the plant had been properly maintained and improved.

Only a year earlier the company had reported a profit and the shareholders seemed happy. It looks like a remarkably sharp change in fortunes.

The following month the Court decided that Samuel Lowell Price, of Price, Holyland and Waterhouse, should act as the official liquidator with James Williams as his local representative. The manager was given permission to carry on production but brewed only 400 barrels a month until January 1867 when the figure dropped to around 200 barrels.

End of an Era

Once the liquidator got to work the scale of the financial problems became clear. Rather than producing a profit of £4500, as they had in the first year of trading, they had incurred a loss of £10,000. By the end of the year this had increased to £20,000. In the opinion of Mr Price the directors had not kept a close enough eye on proceedings. The capital raised had been £60,000, but half had already vanished, and the five largest creditors were claiming £4000 each in addition to which there were further liabilities of around £32,000.

On 27 July 1867 the brewery was put up for auction but not a single bidder was to be found and the business was closed down. In the circumstances this is hardly surprising although the plant was modern and the little empire of public houses sensibly organised.

The disaster seems to have been quite unforeseen. Significant building work and the installation of new plant had to be financed but even so the transformation looks almost bizarre. Sadly there seems to have been no coherent business plan and no alternative strategy to retrench and form a profitable baseline. The directors clearly hoped that the second year would bring the breakthrough they were looking for but when that did not happen they had no alternative but to put the brewery into liquidation.

For most shareholders this meant a loss of about £1000. However, for the Barnes Company and its members the loss was nearly £10,000. For Lloyd Baxendale of Pickfords the loss was even greater. He had taken 100 shares and so lost the sum

Ring of Fire

At some point in the 1880s the Ship Inn at Morcombelake, a pub leased to the Old Brewery, was burnt down. The tenant travelled to Bridport the following day to explain what had happened. He claimed that he had lost everything, including the pub's cash box, and all that he had left was some clothes. The brewery owner, Mr Job Legg, was suspicious. Why save clothes rather than money, particularly as the tenant owed a month's rent on the pub? Mr Legg decided to send his builder Mr Brooks and a couple of other men down to the site to sift through the debris and see if they could find the cash box. He said that if the box was found then the debt would be written off.

In fact Brooks did find the cash box exactly where the tenant said it would be and inside it were between 12 and 20 gold sovereigns and several silver coins too – enough to settle the debt. However, the coins had got so hot in the fire that they had all been welded together into one solid lump. The valuable lump stayed in the brewery manager's desk drawer for some time until Mr Legg decided to give it as a gift to Mr Stickland the brewery manager and his son, who also worked in the office. In the end the coins were cashed in at the bank, all except one, which was mounted on a chain (pictured above) by Mr Matthew the local jeweller. Today the chain remains with the Stickland family.

of £10,000 on his own account. Sadly, the worst affected was Samuel Bowden Gundry. He had seen the brewery develop since the partnership of 1832 and watched it gain a good reputation for its beers both nationally and internationally. He lost his £10,000 shareholding as did Baxendale but he also had double that amount in the form of a mortgage with the brewery.

Mercifully Samuel Bowden Gundry did not live to see the final closure of the brewery, he died in July 1867. Subsequently nearly all his relations left Bridport, his sons Henry and Frederick moving to London. Henry later joined the Church and obtained a living in Monmouth though he did finally return to Dorset late in life.

After its collapse in 1867 the Old Brewery came into the hands of the Leggs, a well-established farming family from Litton Cheney. The Leggs, however, never really seemed to come to terms with the business. Though one lasting symbol of their involvement in the business was the installation of the brewery waterwheel, which is still in use today. The waterwheel was forged in Bridport by Mr Thomas Helyer in 1879 from a design by General Poncelet, who was one Napoleon's generals in the Napoleonic Wars. The wheel's diameter is 18 feet, weighs 6 tons and its optimum speed is 10 rpm, giving a flange speed of 6½ miles an hour.

After a while, and the deaths of two generations of the family, the brewery was run by Edward Cox with the assistance of a couple of Legg executors, Stephen Whetham and Charles Nantes. Things were not going well and in November 1893 the executors and Cox received a report from their advisers on the running of the brewery, together with the figures for the last ten years. It told them to chase debts and reduce stocks of spirits and barley. Yet again financiers suggested that the brewery ought to be sold as soon as possible to avoid further accumulation of debts. The Leggs seem to have been no more successful at running the brewery than their immediate predecessors.

Top right When the brewery closed in 1867 ownership passed from the Gundrys to the Leggs, another important local family. Job Legg, seen here leading a parade on his tricycle, was the brewery's new owner.

Bottom right This waterwheel, which replaced an earlier one, was installed in 1879 and provided power for a number of pieces of the brewery's machinery. Mains electricity came to Bridport in 1930 and from then the waterwheel slowly became redundant as a main source of power, but it is still in working order today.

The Palmers of North Perrott

After these failures the prospects for any new brewer in West Dorset seemed dim indeed. In 1896, however, the Palmer family established a new brewing company, which has continued as an iconic local enterprise for more than a hundred years and is still going strong at the beginning of the twenty-first century.

The Palmers are an old established Somerset family from the North Perrott area near Yeovil. John Palmer (1770–1828) farmed near the village of Huish Episcopi until the outbreak of the Napoleonic Wars. He then joined the Royal Navy and served as Lieutenant on HMS *Edgar* in 1805–6 after which he was promoted to Commander and then Captain. Around 1811 he moved his wife, Ann, and two girls, Ann and Mary, to Plymouth where two sons, John and Robert, were born. After the end of the war in 1815 he moved back to Somerset, farming at Thornfalcon near Taunton. Here his family was completed with the birth of Edmund Cleeves and Jane. When Captain John died in 1828 the family were in straitened circumstances and his widow had to appeal to King George IV

Opposite **The start of a dynasty: Cleeves Palmer with his three surviving children in 1894 – Leslie (left), Bob (standing) and Eddie – around the time he bought the Old Brewery in Bridport.**

for help. She wrote, 'In an interview my late husband had with His Majesty, he was pleased to say in view of his service testimonials, His Majesty would be a friend to his children for life.' King George IV's response is not known, but what is known is that all of his children were educated and that his widow was never short of money again. His wife eventually moved back to North Perrott where she died in 1839.

Robert (1815–1895), the fourth Palmer child, married Elizabeth Ellen Pring around 1850 and was farming at Holway, just to the south of Taunton when their first child, Elizabeth Mary, was born in 1853. Their first son John Cleeves, who was to be known as Cleeves, was born the following year. A year or so later the family moved to the Manor, West Bexington, on the Dorset coast where a second son Robert Henry, known as Henry, was born in 1867.

In 1880 Robert Palmer approached Henry King, owner of the Odiham Brewery in Hampshire, with an offer to buy the beer-making side of the business. King, whose grandfather had started the operation in 1790, was keen to sell and Robert bought the business for just under £30,000 installing his son Cleeves as a partner in the renamed company, King and Palmer. King was 66 years old but continued to run the family farm, which included its own hop garden, while Cleeves, 40 years his junior, ran the brewery.

Odiham Brewery was a small country eight-quarter brewery employing 12 men, some of whom also worked on King's farm. When Cleeves arrived the brewery was selling 2500 barrels per year, producing an income of £5690. The company also produced most of its own malt and hops. Gradually Cleeves built up the trade and by the time he married King's daughter, Eliza, in October 1887 the brewery was producing 3200 barrels a year and had an income of £7676.

Cleeves and Eliza had four children of whom the eldest, Henry Robert Cleeves, was born in 1888. The business continued to thrive with the income reaching £9143 in 1892, the year after Henry King's death. However, tragedy was not far around the corner for Eliza died in childbirth in March 1894. Her infant son died a few months afterwards.

Around October 1894 the recently widowed Cleeves was offered a chance to buy the Old Brewery in Bridport. He was tempted because it was a step up the scale but he still had to weigh up his options. The Odiham business was small but profitable. Cleeves was the only wines and spirits merchant in the area and was also making his own mineral waters. As well as the brewery there was a freehold estate of 15 full licensed houses, three beer houses and one off-licence. Another two fully licensed houses and three beer houses were leased. The brewery had its own malthouse and 28 acres of hopfields, 11 acres of which were freehold with two oast houses as well as a farm and a number of cottages. Cleeves was willing to sell it all for £31,750, and in May 1895 a firm offer was received from Harry P. Burrell, owner of Crowley and Co., the Alton

Brewers. Odiham Brewery became part of Crowley's on 1 October 1895, six months after Cleeves and his brother Henry took control of the Old Brewery in Bridport. The brothers had already decided to work as partners in a private partnership, rather than as a limited company.

On 30 March 1895 their father Robert died and a few months later Cleeves moved from Hampshire to join his younger brother in Bridport. He rented a house at 29 South Street from Maria Whetham and from 30 September he was very much the senior partner operating a hands-on policy on the site.

Despite the Odiham sale they needed more cash because Bridport cost over £82,000 compared with the £30,000 they had got for Odiham. In the end the bulk of this was covered by mortgages to the Legg family or their executors.

The partnership made Cleeves the senior partner with five of the nine shares but it was not until 1897 that the profits were divided on this basis. The initial capital put in was £17,250 by Cleeves and £13,250 by Henry but the balance of profits in the first year was divided equally to reflect the work put in by each brother. Now, at last, the business – J. C. and R. H. Palmer – was finally under the new management of John Cleeves and Robert Henry.

Above Loading the dray with barrels in the Old Brewery yard, 1890s.

The 1890s, however, were not prosperous years in rural England and the outlook in and around Bridport was bleak. Agriculture was depressed and remained so until the beginning of the Great War in 1914. In Bridport itself there was also a lack of confidence in the local staple textile trade, and especially rope and net making. This reflected a national trend but was exacerbated by a crisis in Newfoundland with which the town had always enjoyed a significant trading partnership. Bridport supplied most of Newfoundland's fishing nets. In 1898 things got so bad that two of the town's best-known net manufacturers, Whethams and Tuckers, went out of business altogether.

Trading conditions in the textile industry improved a little thanks partly to the Boer War (1899–1902), which prompted an increase in demand for forage nets for cavalry horses. But the situation in the harbour area of West Bay was particularly depressing. Shipbuilding was in decline and consequently the little port's population halved between 1870 and 1901 to a mere 250 inhabitants.

Despite this Cleeves and Henry Palmer were determined to forge ahead. They celebrated Queen Victoria's Diamond Jubilee in 1897 by marketing crates of a dozen bottles of Palmers Best Bitter for just 1/6d. Other measures were more mundane. After the takeover, for instance, one of the first things the firm did was to put a corrugated iron roof over the yard to provide weather protection for the workforce and to build a new mineral water plant. This building cost £110 and was fitted out for a further £337. It was money well spent for almost immediately the brewery

Opposite The purchase order for the Old Brewery as bought by Cleeves and Henry Palmer in 1896.

Above The people of Bridport took to the streets in honour of Queen Victoria's Diamond Jubilee in 1897. Many celebrated by toasting the monarch with bottles of Palmers Best Bitter brewed specially for the occasion.

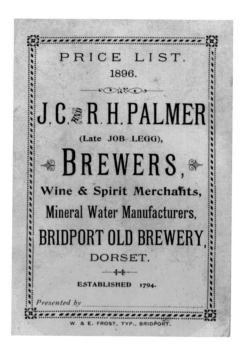

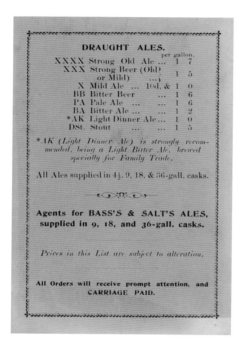

started to make a profit of between £500 and £1000 a year. Henry King, son of the
former owner of the Hampshire brewery, was brought down from Odiham to
become the brewery manager at a salary of £108 a year and was given a staff of three,
which included head brewer G. G. Richardson, Edward Cox and John Stickland.

The year after their acquisition the Palmers built improved office accommodation
and converted the old stables by the main gates as well as installing a block floor and
counters with heating. Palmers also introduced the sale of bottled beer. Cleeves
purchased bottled Pale Ale and Stout from other brewers at first. This proved so
successful that he installed his own beer bottling line in the autumn of 1897, with a
six-syphon bottling machine. The beer was bought in casks, initially from Salt and
Bass but later from Marstons and Guinness. Palmers also bought some Prince's Ale.
Worthington's Pale Ale and 'E' were added in 1906 and the firm was an early
entrant into the lager market with the purchase of Jacob's Pilsener and Allsopp's
bottled lagers from 1904.

The early days of Palmers ownership saw some fundamental changes in drinking
habits. Outdoor leisure pursuits, such as football, cricket and golf, took some of the
disposable income previously spent on beer. There was the popular Bridport

Horticultural and Cottage Garden Improvement Society, which interfered with long hours in the public bar. There was also an upsurge in the temperance movement, which inevitably meant an attack on the brewing industry.

In December 1899 Henry Montgomery took over from G. G. Richardson as head brewer. Born in Coventry in 1853 Montgomery married in Birmingham during 1874 and was an under-brewer in Oldbury-on-Severn by the following year.

Opposite The Palmers Brewery price list for 1896.

Above South Street in Bridport, a street in which every other house was reputed to be a pub, also attracted the temperance movement and the Quakers set up this poor house to provide shelter for the victims of the 'demon drink'.

Before taking up his position at Bradford he worked for breweries at Norton Fitzwarren, Taunton and for Crewkerne United Brewery.

Minor alterations in the brewing plant continued with the most significant being the introduction of a Morton 40-barrel refrigerator in 1901. This replaced two old coolers, which were offered for sale. In 1897 the old dome copper was fitted with a steam heater; a new mash tun was installed in 1907 and the old boiler was replaced by a state-of-the-art Galloway Flue Boiler in 1910. The malt mill and screen was renewed in 1912.

Even then the business was not solely dependent on brewing for its income. Palmers also ran a successful wines and spirits department and, while the sale of spirits remained stable at around £6500 throughout the period, the income from wine sales gradually increased from £200 in 1896 to around £500 by 1914. Private clients accounted for about half of all sales of wine.

West Dorset has always enjoyed healthy cider sales. Even as far back as the first half of the nineteenth century a good apple crop made the local brewers fear for their beer sales the following year. Normally tenants of public houses purchased their supplies of cider directly from local farmers. The drink had the advantage of being cheap due to having either very low or non-existent levels of duty. It was therefore difficult for brewers to purchase from the larger cider makers and make a profit. However, from 1905–6 Palmers purchased small amounts of cider first from Quantock Vale Cider and then Hills Cider of Staverton in 1909–10.

The temperance movement was a continual thorn in the Palmers side. Bridport had a significant Nonconformist Society and this had a marked influence on trade. All breweries were under pressure to reduce the number of licensed houses. Bridport had around 50 houses serving a population of 10,000, which meant a ratio of one house to 200 people. The temperance reformers wanted the figure to be nearer one house per 1000. This would have meant the closure of almost 40 licensed houses in the Bridport area alone.

In 1903 the local magistrates, of whom Cleeves was one, pressed the brewery to close a number of houses voluntarily and as a result six were closed – most of them owned by Palmers. Often the houses closed were within a few yards of another so the overall effect on trade was minimal. Even so Palmers had to pay a Mr Tucker of the Avenue £200 as compensation for loss of trade.

The Tory government reacted to widespread pub closures with a Licensing Bill in 1904, which meant that brewers could be reimbursed for the loss of licences unless

they were lost because of unruly behaviour or drunkenness. Under this legislation several Palmers houses were closed. In 1908 the Rose in Bridport's West Street closed for business and Palmers were infuriated when no compensation was offered. It had been a beer house and grocer's shop for many years but after the

Above West Street was the site of a number of pub closures following the Licensing Bill in 1904.

death of the licensee no successor could be found and the house was run under management. The Compensation Authority gave an award of £201 but the Revenue didn't agree. Despite protests they stuck to their guns and Palmers eventually gave up chasing the money.

No further closures took place until 1912 when the George at Lyme Regis and the Nag's Head in Bridport were shut down followed by the New Inn, also in Bridport,

the following year. In 1914 Palmers made almost £2000 from the sale of redundant houses. Basically they knew they had too many houses and saw the need to rationalise them.

Cleeves, a Tory, campaigned actively against the Liberal government which had won power from the Conservatives in 1906 and which was more hostile to the brewers than his own party. He took an active role in campaigning against Liberal legislation. A bill he considered inimical to the brewers was passed in the Commons but the industry saw its chance for revenge in the Tory-dominated House of Lords. Cleeves organised about 150 local people to attend a big protest

Opposite The Ship Inn, South Street, in 1910. In order to keep profits up the Beer family ran two adjoining establishments. Mr Beer ran a saddlery business in one part of the building while his wife Sarah ran the pub.

Above By the turn of the twentieth century J. C. and R. H. Palmer was a well-established business, brewing and selling a range of beers and mineral water as well as importing and selling a wide variety of wines and spirits.

The West Bay Skittle Club

The West Bay Skittle Club was officially founded in 1908. A skittle club had existed for a few years by then having originally been set up by Norman Good in the stables of his West Bay business. Good was born in 1880 and had founded a highly successful sand and gravel business. His ancestors had acted as Lloyd's agents since 1828. The site of the stables that had been converted into a skittle alley is now used as two shops. The informal club was originally made up of a group of friends from the farming and business communities. There were breaks during these skittle matches so that the 'sticker-up' (the person who stands the skittles up when they have been knocked down), a certain Harry Hawkins, could be despatched to the nearby West Bay Hotel in order to bring back refreshments, mostly pints of Palmers ale.

It wasn't long before Good decided to approach Cleeves Palmer and enquire whether he would be prepared to put up a permanent alley at the West Bay Hotel. The answer was in the affirmative and the club was formally established in time for the 1908–9 season. In the early days there wasn't a bar in the alley and so members wishing to order drinks had to blow down a pipe (similar to the system used

West Bay Skittle Club in action – as traditional as a pint of Palmers ale.

on ships). This would alert a member of staff in the bar and they would come down to take the drinks order.

The Goods and the Palmers have maintained their cordial relationship since the club began. Founder Norman Good died in 1936, the year after his son Geoff joined. He was secretary from 1947–77 and treasurer from 1977–2000 and remains an honorary member to this day; while a Palmer has been president ever since Cleeves agreed to provide a home for it: Cleeves himself from 1908–28, Bob from 1928–71, Tony from 1971–86 and John from 1986 to the present day. Many of the early members have had sons, grandsons and even great grandsons follow them into the club including local farmer Ralph Wyatt who joined on the same day as Geoff Good in 1935. It is a truly family affair.

meeting in London at the end of September 1908. The Bridport contingent travelled by train from Bridport railway station. Some 150,000 attended the meeting at which 70 speakers made speeches from 20 platforms.

The outcome was a defeat for the government in the Lords. The Liberals retaliated by putting forward a swingeing budget the following year. This increased the prices of the licenses needed for brewing and for retail. Once again it passed through the Commons but fell in the Lords. Fed up, the government went to the country in 1910 and were re-elected. A new Licensing Act was passed but without the more extreme measures of its predecessor.

One of its provisions, however, was to haunt Palmers in future years. A Hotel Licence required that less than one third of its income should be from drinks. The new government also passed the Parliament Act in 1911, which limited the powers of the Lords to defeat Government Bills. The result was that Palmers licences increased from under £100 to over £300. In common with other brewers Palmers reacted by contesting the new rate values but without success.

This period of expansion closed with the outbreak of war in 1914. During the 19 years since the Palmers took over, profits averaged £13,782 a year. They rose gradually to a peak of £15,000 in 1904. These were good results considering the difficult times but they were only achieved by prudent and cautious management.

The Perils of War

In common with many other towns in England West Dorset was heavily affected by the Great War. One hundred and fifty men from Bridport and the surrounding area perished in the conflict and almost every horse was commandeered by the forces. On the plus side the rope and netting industries thrived due to the demand for everything from hammocks to tent-lines and local volunteers made 130,000 surgical dressings for field hospitals. In a symbolic gesture the King of Prussia public house was renamed the King of the Belgians in recognition of the Belgian refugees that the town was housing, many of whom were working in the town's factories and contributing to the war effort. The *Bridport News* stated, 'Nowhere in the country is the patriotic spirit more marked, now that the perils of war have burst upon the country, than in Bridport.'

The conflict inevitably had an effect on Palmers Brewery. For a start the enlistment of so many men into the armed forces reduced the number of beer

Oppposite A procession in honour of the coronation of King George V wends its way down Victoria Grove and into West Street on 23 June 1911. It was the last major celebration on the streets of Bridport before the onset of the Great War three years later.

drinkers in the neighbourhood quite drastically. By January 1916 some 1600 men had joined up from the Bridport area, with more than half of them coming from the town itself. Conscription, introduced later in the year, added to this figure significantly. To make matters worse whereas other Dorset brewers could fall back on the number of beer-drinking troops stationed in their areas, Bridport remained a troop-free zone for most of the war.

However, there was full employment in the town for the duration because the local factories were engaged in war work but it became increasingly difficult to find suitable able-bodied tenants for public houses. They were all at the front or engaged in essential jobs connected with the war. A third of the brewery's 'waged' workforce went to war, resulting in a fall in numbers from 20 in 1914 to 13 in 1916, though clerical staff were not so greatly affected with only one man apparently called up. To make matters worse the government imposed restrictions on brewing beer, especially from 1917. Shortly afterwards they introduced price controls as well.

Palmers' production slumped to 70 per cent of the pre-war levels in the year ending June 1917. Only just over 6000 barrels were racked. Because of this the brewery had capacity to spare and between April and September 1916 approaches were made to a number of other breweries offering to help them out. Devenish of Weymouth responded by asking Palmers to brew 250 barrels for use in their local military canteens. When Devenish were asked to provide the raw materials and casks, which were both in limited supply in Bridport, they said no. Palmers came back with an offer of 200 barrels at a profit of 13 shillings per barrel, but this too was rejected.

Britain imported 80 per cent of its cereals and this led to incessant attacks by German U-boats seeking to starve the country into submission. The first local victim of German submarines was HMS *Formidable*, which was sunk in 1915. The bodies of crewmembers were brought ashore at Lyme Regis and laid out on the floor of a Palmers house – the Pilot Boat Inn. The landlord owned a collie called Lassie and as the dog was moving around the makeshift morgue she

Opposite In common with their colleagues the First World War had an enormous effect on the lives of the schoolboys of Bridport. Many lost their fathers and all were forced to grow up quickly and take up the challenges of manhood before they were ready.

Above The Pilot Boat Inn, Lyme Regis, was the birthplace of the story of the collie dog Lassie.

suddenly licked the face of one of the 'corpses' whereupon the body rose, as it were, from the dead and revealed itself as still very much alive.

Cleeves Palmer became Bridport Mayor for the third time in November 1916. The Defence of the Realm Act meant that there was much to do. Luckily he had a staunch deputy in E. S. Reynolds who was able to take on much of this work for him. During Cleeves's mayoralty the War Savings Committee, of which he became chairman, was set up and by the end of the conflict had raised some £620,000 worth of War Loans, one of the highest sums in the county. In some ways Bridport was in a fortunate position as it had full employment during the war even if the brewers suffered from a lack of thirsty troops in the area. The reduction in beer sales probably had more to do with the loss of customers than with the price increase, which saw a pint doubling to 4d. Palmers instituted quotas of supply on all their houses. Like their own production it was based on pre-war figures, which were calculated on a monthly basis. From August 1917 Palmers frequently had to tell their landlords that they had exceeded their quotas. At the same time the brewery kept a reserve of beer for emergencies and landlords who had completely run out were

The Lassie Story

The story of Lassie made the national press and must have been noticed by Eric Knight, a Yorkshireman who had relocated to Hollywood to work as a scriptwriter. He published a short story in the *Saturday Evening Post* in 1938 about a collie who crossed hundreds of miles of rugged terrain to return to the boy she loved. Two years later a novel, entitled *Lassie Come Home*, was published to huge critical acclaim. So it's true to say that a Palmers house played host to the beginning of a virtual industry of 'Lassie' books, films and television series.

Able seaman John Cowan and Lassie, the dog that saved his life after the sinking of HMS *Formidable*.

Opposite Cleeves Palmer, Mayor of Bridport, as depicted in this portrait which hangs in the Old Brewery boardroom to this day.

often allowed a 'kilderkin' or two from the Palmers reserve. By March 1918 even this had run out and at times there was simply no beer. As late as March 1919 Palmers were complaining to the Food Controller that their houses were having to close on a number of days each week because they had run dry.

In an attempt to eke out the supplies of Best Bitter the landlady of the Angel at Lyme Regis was advised to sell it only by the 3d glass of which there should be at least five to the quart, equivalent to 7½d per pint. There wasn't enough to sell it in pint glasses. An alternative approach was to offer mild in lieu of bitter with one barrel of bitter being equal to two barrels of mild. This would at least give the tenants a little more beer to sell even though it was very weak. Serving a combination of beers that sold at different prices was forbidden in 1917. As a result Palmers advised Mr Prescott, the landlord of the Ship at Lyme, to sell the 4d mild and the 5d bitter in different glasses and allow the customers to mix them for themselves.

Sales of spirits in public houses fell by about a third during the war though private sales fluctuated and were more complicated. The government introduced restrictions on the strength of spirits sold over the counter and as a result Palmers had to circulate their houses in June 1916 advising them to dilute their spirits with cold boiled water: one pint of water to every gallon of spirits. In May 1918 Palmers registered their Golden Cap brands of Irish and Scotch whisky with the Ministry of Food. These were their own blends of superior, more-than-five-year-old whiskies and had been blended by the brewery for over 50 years.

Compulsory enlistment was obviously disruptive to the brewery and to the tenants' families who were consequently forced to move. To prevent this the Chief Constable of Dorset allowed licences to be transferred temporarily to the family of the tenant for the duration of the war. The first recipient of such a licence was Mrs Atkins of the Pilot Boat at Lyme Regis. Her husband was called up in 1916 but she took over the licence – and Lassie – with immediate effect.

Bridport accepted a number of Belgian refugees during the war, beginning with a group of 40 who settled in the town and found employment in local factories. A fund was also set up to help them. As a thank-you for this effort the King of Belgium conferred on Mayor Cornick the King Albert Medal and his wife was given the Medal of Queen Elizabeth. George Nantes was awarded the Golden Palm Medal. It was this Belgian connection that was partly responsible for Palmers renaming their pub the King of Prussia and calling it

the King of the Belgians in July 1915. (The pub was renamed the Lord Nelson in 1940 when Leopold III, then King of the Belgians, was removed from office by the invading Nazis.)

Only two licensed houses were added to the estate during the war. The first of these was the Crown Inn, Puncknowle, which had been leased since 1899. The other acquisition was the Loders Arms in 1916 following the sale of the whole of the Loders Estate.

Delivery of beer to the houses was still carried out by horse drays. At the start of the war there were eight horses hauling the drays. Later the Army took a number to work in France and in 1917 only five horses remained to do the heavy roadwork. This wasn't enough so in the following year Palmers asked permission to buy four replacements. Motor drays were not used until August 1919 when a lorry from Pinney's Roller Mill at Lyme Regis was hired on Fridays during the season.

Above East Street, Bridport. The pub third on the right, the King of Prussia, was renamed as the King of the Belgians for a time in honour of the Belgian refugees that lived and worked in the town during the conflict. It was later renamed the Lord Nelson, the name it retains today.

Old Bottles and Stone Jars

In the early days of brewing, bottles used cork stoppers to keep the contents fresh. But these corks were not effective unless they were wet. Bottles were often made with round bottoms (bottom) so that they could not be kept upright and the liquid would keep the corks wet during storage.

Another innovation was needed to keep carbonised drinks, such as aerated water, from blowing corks out in storage. In 1875 Hiram Cod invented the 'cod' bottle (right). These bottles had a glass marble in the top that created a seal when the bottle was turned upside down and the marble pressed against a gasket or rubber ring. Palmers only used these bottles for soft drinks and they were phased out not long after the Great War.

The large stone jar (below) would have been used for spirits. It would have been filled with the Golden Cap range of spirits in the brewery and delivered to the pubs for sale to the landlords' customers. The smaller stone jar (below right) would have been filled with the Palmers range of cordials and squashes including lime, blackcurrant and peppermint cordial along with orange, lemon and grapefruit squash.

Two of Cleeves' sons died during the war, Edmund (Eddie) was educated at Sherborne School before becoming articled to an accountant. He worked for Mason and Sons, accountants to the brewing trade, including the Old Brewery. In August 1914 he was turned down for active service owing to poor eyesight. Instead he joined the 'Friends' Ambulance' in France. He later returned to England, gained a commission in September 1915 and joined the Nelson Battalion of the Royal Navy Division. After training he was sent to France in February 1917. He was fatally wounded on 23 April, dying of his wounds two days later.

Leslie, the second of Cleeves's sons, was also educated at Sherborne. He then learned his trade as a brewer before taking up a position as junior brewer at Cobbold's Brewery in Ipswich. Like his brother Edmund he failed his medical at the start of the war but was commissioned in July 1915 in the 4th Dorset Regiment and was attached to the Machine Gun Corps, going to France in June 1916. He was gassed there and invalided home in October. After recuperating he returned to France in June 1917. He was killed by a sniper during the second phase of an attack on 20 September 1917 after pushing to within 50 yards of the opposing infantry. He was buried where he fell; just east of Shrewsbury Forest, 2½ miles east of Ypres.

Cleeves's eldest son, Henry Robert Cleeves, known as Bob, was working for Adnams brewery in Southwold, Suffolk as head brewer. In October 1914 he married Elsie Smorfit of Barnsley whom he had met while working at the Barnsley Brewery. Bob was called up for military service in May 1918 but was back at Southwold in November of the same year.

All the old brewery men who joined up were given guarantees of future employment on their return. All but one returned safely. The sole fatality was George Rawles, who had enlisted in August 1916, and was killed in France during the last month of the war. Not all the survivors came back to work at the brewery but where possible they were replaced by men who had done military service.

The staff of the Palmers brewery often remained for many years. One such person was John Stickland who retired from his position on his golden wedding anniversary in July 1915. He was given an extra month's salary as a bonus. The son of a Bridport shoemaker he trained as an accountant before joining Gundry Downe and Company in 1857. He rose to become a trusted and much valued employee, guaranteeing the bond for the spirits warehouse until his death just two years after his retirement. At his funeral at Bothenhampton he was borne to the grave by six bearers from the brewery – a symbolic gesture, which illustrates that Palmers were a family business in more ways than one.

Opposite Two of Cleeves Palmer's sons were killed during the Great War. Edmund (top) died of wounds on 25 April 1917, while Leslie (below) was shot by a sniper at Ypres on 20 September the same year.

Above Cleeves's eldest son, Henry Robert Cleeves but known as Bob, married Elsie Smorfit on 8 October 1914. They are pictured here with their two sons, Tony (left) and Cleeves.

Peace

A ny hopes of Palmers Brewery returning to the trading conditions that operated in the pre-war years were soon dashed. After the end of the war in 1918 there was a short-lived boom caused by the relaxing of wartime restrictions, but by 1921 there was widespread industrial unrest as Britain struggled to restore its pre-war export links. Many trading relationships, especially those involving cotton and coal, were never to return to their previous levels as other countries had taken Great Britain's place. Bridport may have seemed isolated from the depression that began to settle on the nation, but the miners' strike of 1921 had an impact as many of the town's industries relied on coal-generated steam or gas for power.

The sudden fall in coal sales in 1925 was partially responsible for the General Strike of the following year. Although all but the miners returned to work after two weeks, coal sales continued to fall, from 73 million tons in 1913 to 39 million

Opposite Though trading was tough for many local industries during the inter-war years Palmers Brewery was at its peak in many ways. With a stable workforce and a local customer-base the Brewery was able to expand its business in a number of innovative ways.

tons in 1932. The return to the Gold Standard in 1925 also made export conditions
worse. Over-production in the USA led to the Wall Street Crash of 1929 and a
worldwide recession, which lasted until 1935. This in turn led to high levels of
unemployment throughout Britain, which peaked at over 3 million in 1932.

Above The brewery has always maintained a bonded warehouse in the locality to store beer,
wines and spirits in optimum conditions. This view shows that there was a healthy appetite for
champagne during the early 1920s.

Conditions in Bridport mirrored those of the nation at large, though a relatively remote corner of rural England was never going to be quite the same as London or Birmingham. Around Bridport between the two World Wars the most spectacular local dispute was a bus-war between new companies determined to establish a crucial link between Bridport railway station and Axminster, the nearest main-line station for London on the Southern Railway between Exeter and Waterloo. If nothing else this emphasised the fact that Bridport and its surrounding countryside was remote and cut-off with communications that were still quite primitive. The movement of commodities such as beer was not easy though this applied as much to imports as exports. It made sense for local demand to be met by local supply and correspondingly it made comparatively little sense for a local brewer to seek markets far from home.

Cleeves Palmer recognised that such ambitions were not only chaotic but of absolutely no benefit to his company and decided to concentrate his efforts in another direction. In March 1925 he held talks with Whiteways, the big Devon cider manufacturers. As a result of this, Palmers started to sell Whiteways cider and cider sales increased 400 per cent on the previous year. Income increased correspondingly and was estimated to have climbed by 243 per cent in the same time frame. From 1925 Palmers took a large volume of cider from Whiteways in order to wipe out the damaging freelance sales from local farmers. The policy worked at first but then the farmers rebelled by slashing their prices and severely undercutting the Whiteways cider. In 1927 Palmers wrote to Whiteways suggesting a lowered price of 16d per gallon to the tied trade and 14d per gallon to the free trade. However, the brewery had located a new income stream, one that was to develop further over the coming years.

Cleeves fell ill with bronchitis in late 1926 and was away from the brewery for some time, during which time his brother Henry took over the day-to-day running of the business. He was ably helped by William Stickland who had taken the place of his father as brewery manager. Cleeves' health did not fully return and as a result Henry spent much of the next year in charge. Cleeves' son Bob was by now an experienced and successful brewer. He began his career working for the Hitchen Brewery during 1907–8 before moving to the Barnsley Brewery between 1909 and 1912. His next position was at Thorne's Nine Elms Brewery in London where his notebook shows that he spent some of the time learning the wine and

Transport

Despite the post-war depression Palmers continued to put its best foot forward. Cleeves bought a copy of a pamphlet called, 'How to make motor transport pay' in late 1920. Shortly afterwards he ordered the company's first motor dray, a 1-ton Ford lorry. George Bonfield & Son of Bridport provided the chassis, with a local firm called Oxenburys adding the body and cab.

It was put on the road in early 1921. Palmers drays were suddenly redundant and by July 1923 only one horse dray was still in service. It continued to make town deliveries until 1949. At least that meant economy and the cost of keeping horses fell from £300 to under £30 a year. By 1924 two Renaults had been added to the fleet and the lorries were being operated from 6a.m. until 5p.m. in the afternoon each day, with the exception of Thursdays, which were half days.

At first fuel for the motorised drays was obtained from Butler Brothers whose garage had been built on brewery land. By 1931 Palmers were using so much petrol that they had to install a fuel tank in the yard.

In 1932 two lorries were repainted in blue with red lines and black wings

Mr Herring drives one of the Palmers drays some time in the 1930s – this vehicle is still kept at the Old Brewery.

together with white lettering. At least one of the other lorries was running in a grey livery at the time. Fleet renewal was started in 1935 with new Ford 1-ton and 30-cwt lorries replacing the Renaults. The following year saw the introduction of the first Dennis, a 50-cwt lorry and the Renaults were sold back to George Bonfield. These lorries were in use until 1945.

spirit trade. In December that year Bob was invited to become head brewer for Adnams. There may have been an element of nepotism about this appointment because his father, Cleeves, was definitely in contact with the Adnams' board at that time. When Bob Palmer arrived in East Anglia there were only seven men working for the brewery and the beer was openly described as indifferent. Bob, however, was a skilled brewer and his success encouraged his father to buy shares in Adnams – a Palmers investment in the East Anglian brewery that continues to the present day.

After a short period of service in 1918 Bob returned to Adnams where he stayed until he was approached by their local rivals Cobbolds in 1924. At both breweries Bob won medals for his beers. But by the time that Cleeves died from bronchitis on 1 May 1928, his son had returned to Bridport in order to run the family brewery in partnership with his uncle Henry. Cleeves had been an extremely talented brewer and businessman and also a shrewd operator who had led the company skilfully during a difficult period for the beer-making industry. His presence at the Bridport brewery was sorely missed.

Above Workmen constructing a bridge over the river behind the brewery pose for the photographer during the 1930s.

The Wine Shop

The Wine Shop in South Street, Bridport, now known as the Book Shop, was first opened in 1836. It was bought by Palmers from W. E. Randall on 4 October 1919 for £2100, the stock cost a further £1537. The Randall family had themselves purchased the shop from the Chick family in 1886. Sadly the shop closed on 30 April 1973, due to the fact that off sales (to take home) had reduced significantly. The last manager was Bert Hibbert who was assisted by two clerks, one cellarman and a driver. The building had wonderful cellars, which supplied private clients and all the brewery's pubs. It has to be remembered that until the mid-1970s wine sales in pubs were extremely small.

Estd. 1794

The Wine Shop

J. C. & R. H. PALMER,
14, South Street,
'Phone 59   BRIDPORT.

In response to an upturn in wine consumption Palmers Wine Store opened in 1985. Located close to the Old Brewery it also serves as an outlet for Palmers ales in draught and bottle. But it also enjoys a growing reputation as a wine merchant of excellence in West Dorset.

Manager Mark Banham, his assistant Luke Machin along with support from Ronnie Mace maintain Palmers traditional approach to service but are also careful not to miss out on innovation when it comes to stock, selecting over 800 Old and New World wines and a wide range of quality spirits to offer their customers. They are also always on hand to offer advice on choice, quality and value.

Estab. 1794

Wines & Spirits
of every description

Famous
Bridport Ales & Stouts
also Mineral Waters

J. C. & R. H. PALMER

THE WINE SHOP
BRIDPORT

There were other developments in terms of business too during the inter-war years. Palmers advertised their beers on local Bridport buses during the late 1920s. Gradually the advertising budget increased as other methods of advertising were employed such as the cinema, local guides and maps. Cozens Steamers, which called at West Bay during the summer months, were also targeted. Even so the annual budget for advertising was usually below £400. In 1933 Palmers signed up to support the national campaign for advertising beer based on the simple slogan, 'Beer is Best'.

In autumn 1931 Palmers sold a small amount of apples to Whiteways, sourcing them mainly from its own tenants, many of whom had small orchards. Two years later Palmers became agents for the purchase of cider apples in the Bridport area. Bob Palmer, whose idea this was, was intent on ensuring that Palmers controlled the local cider business. He wanted to get rid of the tiresome small cider manufacturers who were a thorn in his side. The new policy also meant a small profit for the brewery as Palmers bought apples at £3 per ton and sold them to Whiteways for £4 plus a commission of 18d per ton, although carriage to Whiteways plant at Whimple in Devon had to be deducted from this. Whiteways also offered one replacement apple tree for every ton of fruit sent in.

The brewery first began to take advertising seriously during the 1930s taking space in local newspapers and magazines to promote its wine shop (opposite) and starting a campaign with the simplest of slogans (above).

In December 1932 Henry became ill and was advised to rest, but the following April he died aged 65. He had been a heavy smoker for many years and this no doubt led to his premature death. Henry had been Chairman of the Bridport Rural District Council for 20 years up until shortly before his demise. His interest in the family business was looked after by his executors for the benefit of his widow Octavia, generally known as Evie. However, Evie took no active part in the business and her nephew Bob was now effectively in sole charge.

In the autumn of 1934, Bob made preparations to take over the entire company and transfer the brewery wholly to his own name. In September he wrote to his aunt Evie with a view to buying her husband Henry's share of the business. Aunt Evie had no sons of her own and there was no question of her daughters taking an active part in running the business. By 1935 Bob and Evie had hammered out a mutually acceptable settlement and he was in sole control of the family firm.

Bob's two sons were now being trained to take over in later years. In 1934, his elder boy Robert Leslie Cleeves Palmer (known as Cleeves) started as a pupil brewer with Style and Winch of Maidstone. He returned home to Bridport to enter the family business in 1937. His younger brother Arthur Anthony John Palmer (known as Tony) joined him in 1939 after training at Adnams, his father's old stamping ground.

The inter-war years were tough times for the nation in general and West Dorset in particular. The local twine and net factories continued to decline and by the late 1930s were working a three-day week. Between 1931 and 1935 a textile company called Hounsell's of Bridport even turned to making wooden baskets for the commercial fruit growers in order to combat the worst of the recession. Beer sales too were affected, as drinkers' pockets were not as deep as they wished even though their throats were just as dry.

Henry Montgomery retired from his post as head brewer in September 1936 aged 83. He had spent 37 years in the post; and always refused holidays. He preferred to be paid in lieu. His retirement present for this long-lived dedication was a gift of £50. There was apparently no suitable internal candidate to succeed him so the following March advertisements were placed in trade journals. As a result L. B. Clark, of the High Street Brewery in Maidenhead, Berkshire, was appointed to be head brewer and bottling store manager. However, he turned the

position down on domestic grounds. Bob Palmer was none too pleased by this and
eventually a man called B. N. Thompson was appointed instead.

Under Bob's leadership Palmers continued to increase the number of its licensed
properties. The brewery acquired the Cobb Arms in Lyme Regis (1919); the New
Commercial Hotel (later the New Inn) in Charmouth (1920); the Crown Inn on
West Bay Road and Gollop Arms, Bowood (1922); the Axminster Inn in
Axminster (1923) and the Lily in Bridport itself (1926). In 1926, the copyhold lease
of the White Hart in Beaminster was changed into freehold with a payment to the

Above Tony Palmer (left) and his elder brother Cleeves (third from left) relaxing with friends Jim
Tucker (second from left) and Owen Cooke (right) on board *Yoma* in West Bay, 1936.

Manor of Beaminster. In 1930 the Chideock houses were taken into the freehold estate when the Weld Manor, the estate of an ancient county family, sold off many of its properties. This was followed in 1931 with the sale of the Ilchester Estates' West Bay properties, which included the West Bay and George Hotels. The brewery had leased the former establishment since 1836 so the average outsider would not have noticed any change.

The development of the tourist trade led to two unsatisfactory houses being rebuilt as landmark properties. The Cobb Arms in Lyme Regis was a small house on the road out of the harbour that had been part of the brewery's estate for many years. The freehold was originally purchased in 1919. In September 1935 Bob Palmer wrote to the town council with the suggestion of rebuilding it on a nearby site then occupied by a dilapidated shed and cottage. Mr Homyer, the owner of the site, was prepared to sell and was also interested in buying the old Cobb Arms. The new Cobb Arms was built for a cost of £9000, a small fortune at the time.

The White Bull Inn on Bridport's East Road had been 'improved' in 1929. However, during the mid-1930s Bob Palmer decided that it still wasn't up to scratch to take advantage of the new 'motoring age'. He met the magistrates in February 1936 to discuss the possibility of being allowed to rebuild the house on an adjacent site, which Palmers had bought during the Great War. At the annual Brewster sessions the licence of the White Bull was not renewed until Bob Palmer

and the magistrates had come to an agreement. It was at this time that the name was changed to the Toll House Hotel, reflecting its change in status. The magistrates suggested further modifications in January 1937, including converting the saloon to a restaurant/diner. The idea was to use the stone from the old Netherbury Brewery in the construction of the hotel. Bob Palmer laid the foundation stone on 29 July 1937, the coronation day of King George VI.

It had been intended to rebuild the Coach and Horses in Charmouth at the same time but in October 1936 William Stewart, of the London architects Stewart & Hendry, was told to concentrate on the Lyme Regis and Bridport projects. Further plans to develop a property in West Bay, again using Stewart, were put on hold in May 1938 due to the worsening situation in Europe (Stewart himself was to be killed by a German bomb in the London blitz). However, in 1938 the Bridport Arms Hotel came on the market following the death of its owner Mrs Chorley. The hotel had been held on an annual tenancy for many years and Bob Palmer wrote to ask whether it was to be sold. In November the solicitors wrote enclosing the price wanted for the property. Bob Palmer thought the asking price too high considering that it was not a brewery house. He offered £8000, which he raised to £8500 in March 1939. The offer was accepted and the deeds were transferred in July. By the outbreak of the Second World War in 1939 J. C. and R. H. Palmer were the owners of a well-equipped brewery and a substantial and developing estate.

Opposite Before and after: Bob Palmer felt the White Bull (left) in East Road, Bridport, was not up to scratch despite the improvements carried out in 1929. Further renovations were carried out in 1936 and the pub finally opened as the Toll House Hotel (right) in July 1937. Bob himself (standing just to the left of the sign) and Cleeves (standing just to the right of it) laid the foundation stone.

War Returns

A t the start of the Second World War there was an energetic and
successful Palmer at the helm of the family business with two sons,
Cleeves and Tony, keen to support him. Bob Palmer's elder son Cleeves was
educated at Canford School and, after doing his pupilage at Maidstone,
entered the family brewing business in 1937. On the outbreak of war he
was called up and commissioned into the Royal Engineers. In March 1940,
however, he contracted peritonitis and died on 22 May. He was just 24. Tony,
Bob's younger son, was educated at home after the age of 12. This followed
an emergency trachiometry in his last year at prep school. He then joined
the family business, early in 1939, following a brewing pupilage at Adnams
Brewery. After the outbreak of war in September he too was called up,
joining 483 Searchlight Battery of the Royal Artillery as a Lance Bombardier.

Cleeves's tragic death changed the company's immediate prospects and meant
that Bob Palmer had to run the business single-handedly throughout the war.

Opposite Preparations for D-Day saw an unprecedented 'invasion' of US troops to towns all along
the south-west coast of England. Sights like this one, at Weymouth, were commonplace at West
Bay and other beaches near Bridport.

At one point he even had to act as brewer for the first time in 14 years. He was forced to fire the head brewer, Thompson, because of what were described as 'unpleasant circumstances'. But finding a good brewer in wartime was not easy. He started by interviewing Samuel Reffell Parr in the spring of 1941. Parr had applied for the post in 1936 but failed to get the job. This time he was successful. Bob Palmer described him as 'my sort of brewer'. However, Parr made it clear that his was only a short-term commission and that he would retire as soon as hostilities were terminated.

From September 1939 until the same time the following year significant numbers of troops were billeted in the area, including the West Kent Regiment at 88 East Street, and this resulted in an upturn of business. Other units in the town included the Royal Engineers, the Royal Army Medical Corps and the Royal Artillery. Once they had left the town trade quietened down. In 1941 sales increased again as some Canadian units used West Bay for their training in preparation for the ill-fated Dieppe raid. This operation was intended as a much-needed morale boost for the Allies and was also designed to convince Stalin that Russia was not the only one prepared to make the ultimate sacrifice in order to defeat Nazi Germany. The landings, supported by massive aerial and naval support, were mainly carried out by the inexperienced Canadians. When they finally took place at around five o'clock on the morning of 19 August 1942, many of the hapless young soldiers were machine-gunned as they left their landing craft. A total of 907 were killed and a further 2460 were wounded or captured. This represented about 65 per cent of the total Canadian force of 306 officers and 4658 other ranks.

In many ways the Second World War had the same effect on brewing as the First. Increasing government intervention restricted brewing capacity and beer strength, especially after 1942. This time, however, there was no flourishing temperance

Above As well as running the brewery almost single-handedly during the conflict, Bob Palmer joined the Home Guard to 'do his bit' towards the war effort.

Modern Plant

Made by Wilson & Co from Frome in Somerset, these pine fermenting vessels were added to the brewery in 1939.

During the early part of the war Palmers carried on fitting the brewery with modern plant. In late 1939 two more fermenting vessels of fine New Zealand Kauri pine were introduced, each with a capacity of 35 barrels. The hop back was renewed in early 1940, replacing the unsatisfactory one put in two years earlier. Plans were in place for a new conditioning room, which was to be placed on steel joists above the bottling plant, though only the first stage of this was completed before the end of the war. The steelwork was erected on one side of the bottling plant and four glass-lined steel tanks were also placed there. At the same time a new Victor bottle washing machine was purchased. In 1942 a second-hand steam engine was bought for £60. This Brown and Davis inverted single cylinder engine, No. 6429, is thought to be one of a few still in working order in the early part of the twenty-first century. It is a real museum piece.

movement to threaten the brewers and co-operation between the industry, represented by the Brewers' Society, and the government led to virtually all targets being achieved.

Staffing, both in the brewery and the public houses, obviously posed problems with so many able-bodied men away at the war and the large numbers of young women also deployed in a host of non-combatant roles. A crucial difference this time, however, was that Bob Palmer was determined not to let his skilled staff be called up without serious protest. In 1943 he successfully suggested to the Brewers' Society that the industry should be regarded as 'essential' with the consequence that staff were exempt from conscription. He pointed out that all his labourers had already been taken from him, even when they were over 40 years old, and that

Opposite Palmers managed to retain most of its skilled staff during the Second World War but the general absence of able-bodied men meant opportunities for some women such as this one at work in the wine and spirit bottling store in 1938. Today this serves as the company boardroom.

Above For the first few years of the war the burgeoning tourist industry continued to expand with West Bay being a particularly popular destination, but the advent of bombing and the Blitz in particular ensured that the number of holidaymakers dwindled to nothing by 1942.

Pub Signs

George Biles was born in 1900 and in 1918 he was commissioned to paint his first Palmers pub sign. This began an association between the artist and the brewery that lasted until the year of his death in 1987. He was never happier then when sketching out the designs for a new double-sided pub sign. His research, normally undertaken in Bridport library, was always meticulous.

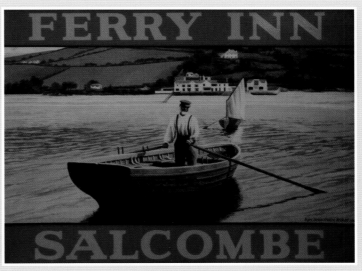

John Palmer remembers many visits to his studio just off East Road in Bridport, in order to cajole him to start the next sign and quite often he had to write out his bills for him and then put a cheque in his hand, otherwise he would never have asked for payment! In his later years Cleeves Palmer arranged for Channel 4 to film George in action, a great tribute to an amazing artist and lovely man.

a further reduction in staff would have been unacceptable. Sense also prevailed in the pubs where the wives of enlisted tenants took over the licences just as they had done in the earlier conflict. All in all therefore Palmers managed to retain a workforce strong enough to cope with demand.

Bridport and its environs had been a backwater between 1914 and 1918 but this was not the case between 1939 and 1945. This time local military activity was sufficient to boost trade. At the same time the presence of so many outsiders placed a strain on the valuable resources allocated to the brewery. Troop concentrations in the area made predicting output significantly more difficult, and seasonal trends in tourism were also a significant factor. The developing tourist industry meant an invasion of thirsty trippers and holidaymakers during the summer months. As a result nearly three times as much beer was brewed in August as in February.

The Battle of Britain and the Blitz brought Bridport much nearer the front line. For the first time the town was vulnerable to aerial attack as well as enemy action at sea. In December 1939 Bob Palmer noted that the population of the town was

Above There were two bombing raids on the centre Bridport during the war, both causing extensive damage, injuries and death.

afraid to go out at night. A few months later he recorded that aircraft were flying over the town each night but that Bridport had been lucky so far. In an attempt to prolong this luck streetlights were not lit from 1940.

But luck was to run out in 1942 when bombs were twice dropped on the town and on both occasions Palmers property was damaged. On the evening of 2 August two Focke-Wulf 190s crossed the coast at West Bay flying at little more than rooftop height and dropped two 500kg bombs on Bridport just after 6.30pm. One scored a direct hit on the Star Hotel in West Street killing four people and injuring a further 19. The second fell into a garden behind the Midland Bank. There was a theory that the Germans' target had been the monumental masons, Appleby and Childs, but this seems unlikely. In fact some of the masons were making top-secret components for the revolutionary Asdic submarine-detecting device. However, the work was so top-secret that even the masons didn't know why they were performing their tasks and it seems extremely unlikely that the Germans knew more than they did. It's much more likely that the Germans were simply jettisoning bombs on the way home.

As a result of the raid the authorities promised a supply of domestic Morrison air-raid shelters and also a light anti-aircraft battery equipped with eight Bofors guns. The battery arrived in September and was in place on 16 December 1942 when a single Dornier 217 dropped a stick of four 500kg bombs on the centre of Bridport, machine-gunned Walditch and escaped across the coast at Abbotsbury. The Bofors guns fired 33 rounds but missed.

Of the four bombs one hit the Westminster Bank but failed to explode. However, inexplicably £919 14s and 6d went missing from the bank (although within two days £898 14s 6d was recovered). The second bomb exploded in the gardens fronting East and King Streets, a third scored a direct hit on houses in East Street and the fourth fell in a meadow opposite East Bridge. Two women and a child were killed; 16 people were injured; three houses were demolished and a further 20 damaged.

Although this was the last time Bridport was bombed, tourism fell away partly because of the danger but partly because the war was dragging on. But for the brewery predicting the level of demand remained a problem. Though the tourists had gone, demand was complicated by the visiting military. Beer consumption ebbed and flowed as the units came and went making it difficult to estimate production levels from one month to the next.

From 1943 until the end of the war the additional presence of evacuees, many
of whom were to work in the local textile industry, also increased sales of beer.
The first evacuees actually arrived within a few days of the outbreak of war but
they were mainly children aged between three and fourteen and consequently had
no impact on the beer business though they did drink mineral waters and fizzy
drinks. Among the 800 billeted in town and the 600 in surrounding villages were
the entire 136 members of the infant class at the senior school in Paddington in
London. At the end of the war just 230 evacuees remained. Not all of them wanted
to go home. They had acquired a taste for rural life.

Above The presence of soldiers in the town had a big effect on the brewery. Ale sales increased
dramatically and the pubs were crowded with many foreign troops preferring to drink with the
locals rather than in their camps.

Royal Visit

King George VI himself came to Bridport early in the war to visit the West Kent Regiment billeted in East Street, and was watched by hundreds of local inhabitants as he and his entourage stopped at the Bull. *The Bridport News* reported the event, although the censor only allowed the paper to reveal that His Majesty had visited 'a well-known seaside resort'. In any event the King and his retinue don't seem to have drunk any beer. Instead 'they had partaken of tea served in a local hostelry'.

The King salutes the people of Bridport as he leaves the Bull (right). They had turned out in their hundreds (below) to welcome the monarch.

The West Dorset area was also a major site for the D-Day preparations and the arrival of extra troops, many of them from the United States of America, led to a huge increase in ale sales. Palmers were asked to supply a number of American camps with beer but also found that the public house trade increased as well. Many visiting troops preferred to drink with the locals rather than in the camps. They left in June 1944 when beer sales dropped again.

Reffell Parr left the brewery towards the end of the war, as had been agreed. He was replaced as brewer by a stopgap named Kempshall who in turn was replaced in March 1948 by Alan Skurray. Skurray had been brewing at the North Kent Brewery in Plumstead and had been a pupil of Bob Palmer's at Adnams. The two had been in contact ever since.

Apart from the difficulty of predicting demand for beer, the war affected drinking and drink production in other ways. Cider sales increased dramatically and stayed high for the rest of the war. These figures do not tell the whole story, however, for as the war progressed the local farmers started to produce their own cider again. Palmers chose to turn a blind eye to their supplying local public houses and 'official' purchases of cask cider therefore fell drastically. In reality, however, cider consumption must actually have increased particularly when the Americans based in the area took to drinking a lethal mixture of cider and beer.

The sales of spirits held up well and yielded an average £18,000 per year at 1937 prices despite restrictions on supplies. Sales of spirits in the glass went down while

Above The first evacuees began arriving in the area during the first year of the war, many of them were children between the ages of three and fourteen like this unknown girl. At the end of the conflict, many of them were not keen to go home having enjoyed country life.

Oppposite West Dorset was a major site for D-Day preparations, particularly for the American forces, and troops were a common sight in the area. The locals took to them and extended their hospitality in many ways.

that of whole bottles increased. Wine bottle sales were negligible and sales of wine by the glass stopped altogether in 1942. Soft drink production was affected by the use of sugar, which was restricted to just 40 per cent of pre-war use. This led to an increase in the use of sweeteners such as saccharine. Once the initial batch of troops moved away the sugar quota was reduced along with everything else. As a result Palmers decided to try out a new artificial liquid sweetener.

Palmers relied on their three recently acquired lorries throughout the war. The vehicles were kept busy, although to reduce fuel consumption deliveries were cut back to just once a fortnight. Lorries only ever left the yard with full loads. Bottled beer was cut back because bottles took up too much space. The drivers were ordered to drive economically which meant travelling slowly. They also had to be back before the blackout started. At the end of the war the Ford lorries were replaced with larger capacity British vehicles. George Bonfield, the local dealer, supplied a 2-ton Austin in July 1945 and a 2-ton Austin in April 1946.

Opposite GIs get a haircut on the beach a few days before the D-Day invasion.

Above With petrol rationed and a blackout in place, deliveries were at a premium during the war years. However, the sight of a Palmers lorry must have brought cheer to war weary locals.

Some outlets though fared badly. The houses hardest hit by the war were the small country pubs where trade often fell severely. At one point it was thought that some of these might have to be closed for the duration of the war but this never happened. To help their tenants Palmers reduced rents, especially where publicans had been hard hit by rate rises imposed by a sometimes hostile-seeming local government.

The hotel trade was not only badly affected by the loss of tourism but also by the requisition of some of the properties. Lyme Regis was the subject of a curfew one hour before sunset, which meant that the catering trade of the new Cobb Arms Hotel was all but killed off. A hotel licence during the war required that alcoholic beverages could not exceed a certain percentage of sales, this was obviously unhelpful. The consequent loss of catering sales and the lower levels of room lettings meant that when it came to the licence renewal the Excise often objected. This happened with the Bridport Arms at West Bay in 1942 and again in 1944

Above Fire rages through the Blue Ball pub in Dottery in March 1947 despite the presence of the Fire Brigade. A new pub eventually took its place, but it took eight years to build.

when the presence of American troops leading up to D-Day led to the closure of West Bay to the public and the requisitions of part of the hotel by the military. The Coach and Horses in Charmouth was similarly affected. A number of pubs in Bridport and the surrounding area were also requisitioned but they were less affected as the tenant could still serve drinks in all of them and this may even have stimulated trade. Palmers beers often contributed to convivial fraternisation and warm Anglo-American relations.

Government bans on repairs caused many problems in the immediate post-war period. For example, a serious fire took place in May 1946 at the Bridport Arms Hotel, damaging the dining room, lounge and front bedroom and resulting in the cancellation of bookings for the Whitsun holidays. Shortly afterwards Bob Palmer was in contact with Adnams, asking for plans of the Swan and the Crown, presumably because he wanted to rebuild the Bridport Arms along similar lines. The hotel was made safe but it was still being described as 'fire-damaged' in 1948.

In March 1947 a fire destroyed the Blue Ball at Dottery. In order to retain the licence and provide accommodation for the tenants, a Nissen hut was erected in its place. This was supposed to be a temporary measure but it was eight years before a new house was built.

Palmers were in a fortunate position by the end of the war. They had a modern plant, which meant that there was little need to invest capital in further improvements. The company was in a strong trading position, especially as it had put money aside to cover the excess profits tax and deferred maintenance demands. In any case restrictions on building that were in force even after the war, permits were needed and these were often difficult to come by.

Bob Palmer had run the business since 1928 and was widely appreciated in the area as tough but humorous. It was said that when he was in one of his pubs, he would always buy a round of drinks, but the drinks had to be Palmers ale.

A new partnership began in July 1947 when Bob Palmer's son Tony joined the business again. He had been appointed assistant brewer in 1939 but had been absent with the Territorials for most of the war. He had married Nora Symonds in March 1946 and they had just produced the first of their six children, Anne, who was born on 1 January 1947. Now he was back the company was poised to move on.

The Age of Change

I It is sometimes forgotten that Britain was in more straitened circumstances in the years following the Second World War than it had been during the conflict itself. Rationing continued for years afterwards. In January 1949 the Labour government cut malt output by another four per cent and ordered a reduction in duty of a guinea a barrel. This didn't help the brewers much because in the same breath the government ordered a price reduction of a penny a pint. This translated into a loss of £7000 for Palmers in the year 1949–50. For a small private company this was money it could ill afford to lose.

From July 1948 beer production at the brewery declined rapidly until April 1949, and then more gradually until December 1949 by which time it was down by 20 per cent. There is some evidence that recovery started around this time but annual production continued to fall until September 1950 when it was at least 25 per cent down on the July 1948 figures. Despite this the motor fleet expanded. In the 1950s the company concentrated on Austins, adding a second-hand A40 pick-up in 1955, a 15-cwt van in 1959 and two 5-ton lorries in 1960 and 1962 respectively.

Opposite An upturn in business in the early 1950s saw an expansion in the Palmers motor fleet.

There were a number of other changes to beer production that had taken place as a result of the war. Oat malt had not been used during the conflict as it was not available. Even after hostilities had ceased the Ministry of Food discouraged its use in production due to continuing problems with its supply. Eventually, in 1949, Oatmeal Stout changed its name to Extra Stout. However, sales of Extra Stout continued to fall in the post-war years until by 1975 it was selling just 60 barrels a year. Stout had simply become unfashionable.

In 1951 the company reverted to crown cork bottles because the manufacturer of the screw top bottles then in use could no longer provide them. In 1961 much of the bottling store plant was renewed and a new tunnel pasteuriser was installed at a cost of over £11,000. Palmers also added an ammonia compressor and refrigeration machine. In the brewhouse the copper was fitted with a Johnson Patent Furnace in 1948. In 1956 the old Galloway boiler was replaced with one from Cochrane's of Scotland. This was put in the original malthouse rather than the brewhouse where its predecessor had been.

Tony's wife Nora was the middle daughter of William Symonds, a partner of Mason and Sons, the company accountants, and a director of the Dorchester brewers Eldridge Pope. The Symonds family were related to the Pope family through marriage. Through this connection, Tony himself was later invited to join the Eldridge Pope board in 1952. Tony and Nora had four daughters Anne born 1947, Susan born 1948, Rosemary and Katherine, who sadly died within hours of being born in 1949. They also had two sons, John who was born in 1951 and Cleeves in 1962.

Bob Palmer was re-elected Mayor in time for the pageant which celebrated the 700th anniversary of Bridport's Charter in 1953, the Queen's Coronation year. Anne, his eldest granddaughter, was invited to present HRH the Princess Margaret

with a bouquet of flowers on her arrival in the town on 21 June 1953. This was a red-letter day for the people of Bridport and they celebrated in style.

Contemporary restrictions on building made it difficult to develop the estate as Palmers might have wished. The bomb-damaged Lord Nelson, for example, was not finally repaired until 1949, seven years after the original raid. Even then Palmers had to appeal after their first application was turned down. The Blue Ball at Dottery fared even worse and was not re-opened for business until 1955. Until then the tenants had to make do with the Nissen hut, which replaced the pub after the fire in 1947. In 1953 the brewery purchased the Three Horseshoes in Burton Bradstock for £8000. The pub had been leased until 1935 and Palmers were delighted to have it back again, this time for good.

Above Mayor Palmer watches as his granddaughter Anne presents HRH the Princess Margaret with a bouquet during the celebrations of the 700th anniversary of the Bridport Charter on 21 June 1953. Henry III originally awarded the charter to the town in honour of its production of rope and netting.

Loyal Staff

Left William Stickland who along with his father John gave almost 100 years service to the brewery.

During the nineteenth and twentieth centuries a number of people gave many years service to the brewery. They included brewery manager John Stickland, who joined *circa* 1856 and worked right through until 1915, and his son William who was employed from 1897 to 1941; George Conway, who joined in 1921 and retired as transport manager in 1962; Bill King, who joined the company in 1930, retired early as spirits manager at the end of September in 1977 due to ill health and sadly died within six weeks.

Ron Hawkins, who had joined the brewery in 1942, completed 45 years service despite ill health in his final years. He was the last employee to deliver beer by horse-drawn dray – a practice that ceased in 1947.

Staff with over 25 years service since 1856*

John Stickland	Henry Montgomery
Ray Major	Henry King
Bill King	Allan Rodway
Tony Palmer	William Stickland
Ernie Chick	J. Cleeves Palmer
Ron Hawkins	Mike Ramsden
Bob Palmer	Andrew Samways
Jimmy Little	Jack Shepherd
George Conway	Audrey Cross
John Palmer	Cleeves (W. R.) Palmer
Peter Fuszard	Alan Skurray
Sid Cross	Freddie Jerrard
J. W. Cross	Jack Burt (PJ)

* names in order of length of service.

Below Ron Hawkins – the last man to deliver Palmers beer by horse-drawn dray.

Above A number of contractors have also worked closely with the brewery over the years. Guy Gale looked after the Brewery's thatched roofs with consummate professionalism for all but 50 years.

In October 1964 Bob and Elsie Palmer celebrated their Golden Wedding. Sadly within ten months Elsie had died at the age of 81. In 1969 both of Nora and Tony's daughters married. In September, Susan married Keith Davis, who a few years later set up the nationally successful Midland Communications company. In December, Anne married Nick Tucker Brown and he became equally successful in his field of property development, specialising in large-scale residential projects.

Bob Palmer retired from running the brewery in 1958. However, he remained a consultant until his death in 1971. Bob had had a long record of public service, which included roles as Chairman of the Bothenhampton Parish Council, President of the Bridport Amateur Operatic and Dramatic Society. He also gave a new wing to the Bridport General Hospital in memory of his elder son Cleeves who had died in 1940. He was a founder member of the Rotary Club of Bridport, President of the Melplash Agricultural Society and Mayor of Bridport in 1936, and again from 1951–53

Tony Palmer remained as sole proprietor until 1976, when the business became a limited company. John, his elder son, had joined the firm in 1969 after extensive training with Whitbread. While the Dorset breweries retained their independence, this didn't happen elsewhere. In neighbouring Somerset, for instance, Arnold and Hancock became part of Ushers in 1955, Brutton, Mitchell and Toms were taken over by Charrington in 1960 and Starkey, Knight and Ford were swallowed by Whitbread in 1962. In Dorset, however, the only merger was between the small Weymouth brewers of John Groves and John Devenish in 1960.

Palmers sales generally followed national trends during this period. Britons seemed to be drinking less beer and across the nation there was definitely a move away from cask beer, which was increasingly

Right Tony Palmer, who originally joined the company as assistant brewer in 1939, took over the running of the brewery in 1958 and remained as sole proprietor until 1976 when the business became a limited company. Here he relaxes at home with his faithful golden labrador Sandy.

considered to be too variable in quality. Low gravity beers were particularly difficult to keep for any length of time, especially in summer. These were the days before temperature-controlled cellars and ale lines.

Another national trend during the 1960s was the move to selling keg beer in place of cask ale. But Palmers stayed true to its tradition, which was to only brew cask-conditioned ales. This was really bottled beer in a metal barrel and needed significant investment. Palmers were not equipped for this. During an 18-month period from 1968, however, all their old wooden barrels were replaced by stainless steel casks which were easier to keep clean and free from infections.

Cooling of the wort was always a problem during the summer months and for many years the company had changed from river water to artesian water for cooling during the summer. In 1962 a 'wort cooler' was purchased from George's of Bristol. A vertical refrigerator was installed the same year. This necessitated the removal of the old cooler room roof where open cast iron coolers were still being used. Four new fermenting vessels were installed in April 1974.

By 1960 all the old beer house licences were phased out and every one of Palmers pubs were operating under a full licence. This change made pubs more appealing to a wider clientele and especially to women who had often felt excluded by the rough male environment of some of the old pubs. Expansion rather than consolidation was very limited until the late 1960s.

In 1965 a site was purchased in Axminster and Palmers used it to build a brand new public house called the Millwey, which was opened in 1967. In 1971 they bought another Axminster pub, the New Commercial Inn. During this period Palmers began to rationalise their pub estate. Too many houses were trading at their historic level of only around 100 barrels a year. This was far too little to make economic sense. It was obvious that there were simply too many pubs in the area and some of them would have to go.

During the 1960s seven houses were closed in Bridport, each one carefully chosen to have as little an impact on popular demand as possible. The Phoenix was shut in 1961 and its customers decamped to the nearby Lily; the Cross Keys was effectively subsumed into the Ship and the George in 1965; and in 1967 the New Robin Hood and the Packhorse were both, in effect, taken over by the Lord Nelson. The Boot and Shoe 'merged' with the King's Head in 1969 and the Sailor's Home was divided between the Five Bells and the Fisherman's Arms in 1970.

Palmers IPA
(Traditional Best Bitter)

Palmers IPA, was added to the range in 1953. For the first five years half the production was bottled while the rest went out in small 'pins' or 'firkins'. By the end of the twentieth century, IPA accounted for over 70 per cent of Palmers ale sales. Palmers overall trading conditions began to improve in around 1958. IPA production increased from 666 to 1621 barrels that year with an average increase of almost 200 barrels annually thereafter.

Today Palmers IPA is still the company's best-selling ale, and is particularly popular right across the south of England.

Adverts for IPA – one of Palmers' finest and most popular brews.

Advertising through the Years

Palmers enjoyed commissioning an array of advertising material to support its ales, wines and spirits and soft drinks all the way through the twentieth century. The images below are representative of the style changes over the years. The two ale-advertising boards (below) were produced in 1936. It is interesting to note that ale prices were the same in the two years either side of that. The other two boards (below right) were produced in 1959. The mineral waters enamelled plaque (bottom left) was produced in 1934, despite no date on the sign, there are a few left in the company archives wrapped in the original newspaper.

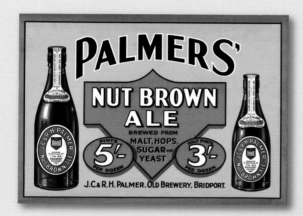

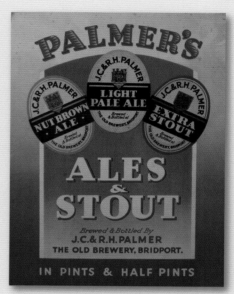

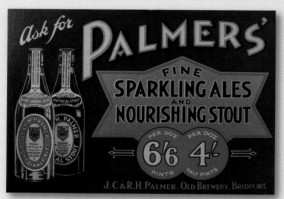

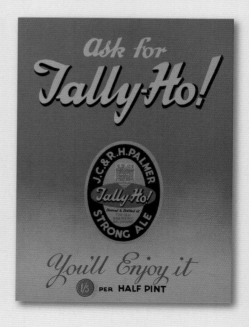

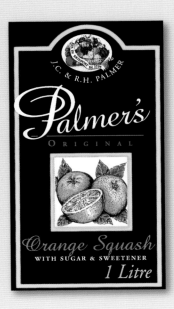

The collection of three Golden Cap labels (top) date back to 1933, also in the range would have been Golden Cap Scotch Whisky and Jamaican Rum. Today only the Golden Cap Gin and Scotch Whisky survive. The name Golden Cap is taken from the highest cliff on the south coast of England, some four miles to the west of the brewery. Golden Cap whisky has been blended in Bridport for well over 100 years. The whisky is created from equal proportions of Glen Grant single malt and North British Distillery grain. The two whiskies are then married together in conjunction with our fine spring water from the Dorset hills.

Palmers range of fruit squashes and cordials were produced until 2007. The squash poster and label (above) were used from the 1950s until the early 1970s; they were then replaced by the typical 1970s style, as shown in the blackcurrant cordial label (above right). This style was in turn replaced in the 1990s with designs similar to the orange squash label (right).

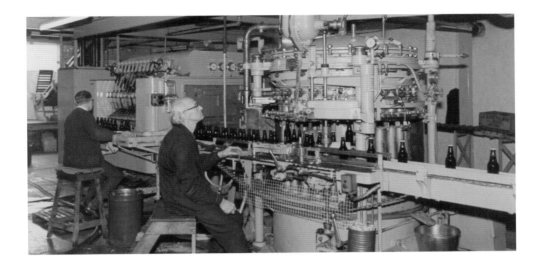

In villages with more than one Palmers pub closures also became the order of the day. Victims included the Sun at Morcombelake in 1965, the Royal Oak in Bothenhampton in 1969, the New Inn at Whitchurch Canonicorum in 1971 and the Farmer's Arms at Loders in 1973. In 1970 West Milton lost its only public house when the Red Lion closed, the first time a village had been left completely without one. Sadly, Palmers judged the pub to be an economic liability.

Sad though drinkers were to see the end of so many pubs, the rationalisation was necessary in the new trading traditions and by 1975 the business was looking streamlined and decently profitable. People were still drinking Palmers beer, which continued to enjoy a good reputation. Cider, traditionally a poor relation, was making a modest comeback. Spirits were steady. But perhaps the most important thing was that Palmers were still a family company with strong West Dorset roots.

Opposite Fundamental changes in British society in the 1960s, partly brought about by the women's lib movement, reminded breweries like Palmers that women were important customers and prompted advertisers to target them specifically as in this charming press ad of the period.

Above With a profitable business and an expanding clientele Palmers upgraded their bottling machinery in the 1970s to keep up with demand.

Carrying on the Family Tradition

T he last quarter of the twentieth century and the first few years of the twenty-first century were interesting times for Britain and for beer. After a dire period of industrial unrest and general depression punctuated by strikes and trades union-dominated disputes, life changed dramatically with the accession to power of a Conservative government led by Margaret Thatcher in 1979. Old-fashioned socialism went in to what still seems like a permanent decline and a rougher, tougher more pragmatic society emerged.

In the 1970s British beer was becoming dominated by nationally produced weak fizzy drinks, widely characterised by serious drinkers as 'flavourless, overtly sweet and uninteresting' and epitomised by mass-produced beverages of little or no character. Palmers continued to produce traditional beers with a distinctive taste, but they were in a small minority and popular fashion appeared to be moving away from the sort of product they favoured.

At the beginning of the decade four beer-loving Manchester journalists founded a grass-roots movement called the Campaign for Real Ale, which had an almost

Opposite John (right) and Cleeves Palmer represent the fourth generation of the family who have run the Old Brewery at Bridport since its purchase in 1896.

unprecedented impact, soon becoming a national institution. It might be overstating the case but after CAMRA's birth, the quality and variety of beer improved out of all recognition, to the great benefit of small independent breweries such as Palmers. Later, the Independent Family Brewers of Britain and the Small Independent Brewers Association did much to enhance the reputation of cask ale. In more recent years a widespread gastronomic revolution also has spread into the nation's public houses. Pubs now produce a quality of food unheard of 30 years ago, when 'scampi in the basket' was the norm. Now some Palmers pubs boast as many as ten fresh fish dishes on their daily menu.

Alan Skurray, who had become head brewer in 1948 and a fine one at that, stayed until his retirement. He had a great sense of humour. On one occasion Skurray put some Epsom salts into a secret horde of bottles that an employee had spirited away for consumption at a later date. Alan often recounted, with much mirth, how effectively the laxative worked causing the dishonest employee frequent visits to the cloakroom that day. Not so many bottles went missing after that. Alan retired in 1974 and was replaced as head brewer by Peter Seed, another man with a reputation as a humourist. Peter had started his career as pupil to his father at the Northampton and Leicestershire Clubs' Brewery. In 1950 he had moved to Lloyds Brewery of Newport and then four years later in 1953 to Starkey, Knight and Ford. Initially he worked at their Bridgwater brewery, before moving to Tiverton in 1964 and on to Bridport a decade later. Peter Seed was an excellent brewer who did much to enhance the reputation of Palmers beer. He retired after 16 years loyal service in January 1990.

Like his father Bob, Tony Palmer gave much of his time to work within the community of West Dorset. He was Chairman of the Bridport Rural District Council from 1968 until it was abolished in 1974. For his services to the St John Ambulance

he was awarded the Order of St John of Jerusalem in November 1973. He was also honoured with the Presidency of the Melpalsh Agricultural Society in 1977. He served as a Justice of the Peace in Bridport for many years and was also President of the Bridport branch of the RNLI.

John Palmer took over as managing director from his father in 1983, the same year that his younger brother Cleeves was elected a director. Cleeves had joined the company three years earlier. During the past 25 years there has been steady growth in both turnover and profits. John's lasting legacy has been in the 'churning of the estate', selling the less good pubs and buying better ones, quite often further afield. It was the advent of food in pubs, in conjunction with families visiting pubs that created the need to change the quality of the pub estate. It was also essential for the company to make purchases away from its heartland of West Dorset. Ten new pubs have been bought in as many years in Somerset and Devon. The core of the business strategy has remained the same throughout and this has been to produce fine ales for Palmers pubs and the company's free trade

Above Head brewer Peter Seed did a great deal to enhance the reputation of the brewery's beer during a time when beer drinkers became more discerning.

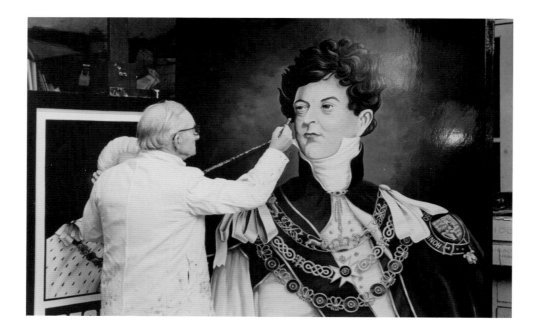

customers. During these years Cleeves has concentrated on developing the free trade business, a part of the business that has grown enormously.

On 19 March 1986, following a few years of ill health, Tony Palmer passed away. He had run the business single-handed through the 1950s until his elder son joined him in the early 1970s. His untimely death at the age of 68 was a great blow to his family; he was a quietly spoken man who was held in great affection by many people. Just before his passing and to his great pleasure, his elder son John concluded an arrangement with the Bridport Sports Trust whereby the Palmer family gave land to the value of £333,000 in Tony's memory, in order to raise funds to build the Bridport Sports Centre. John Palmer concluded the arrangement by leasing eight acres of playing fields to the trust on a peppercorn rent. In more recent times Cleeves has carried on the family tradition, in heading up the re-opening of Bridport's Real Tennis court in 1998 and more recently was much involved in the project to build the new clubhouse at the Bridport & West Dorset Golf Club.

In December 1987 the nationally known pub signwriter George Biles died at the age of 87. He had carried on working right up until shortly before his death. He had painted Palmers pub signs for nearly 70 years beginning with the Hope and Anchor in Bridport in 1927, and his work is still discussed 20 years after his death.

George was a fantastic individual, with a dry humour whose trademark was to paint different pictures on the two sides of a pub sign. A book written by Andy Whipple and Rob Anderson entitled *The English Pub* (1985), is partially dedicated to him with the words, 'To Frederick George Biles, with admiration for his genius'.

In 1989 Tim Woodrow, who had already been with the company for four years and who was already much involved in developing trade in Palmers pubs, arranged for Brian Johnston, the famous cricket commentator, to reopen the Ropemakers in Bridport. Tim, like John and Cleeves, loved the game of cricket and the brothers were delighted when they learned that 'Johnners' would be the man to cut the ribbon on their latest investment. Both brothers still play for the Palmers Cricket Club, which has a fixture list of 20 games each summer.

Opposite Signwriter George Biles worked for Palmers for 70 years. His work can still be seen throughout Dorset and the surrounding counties, often identified by the fact that the signs have a different picture on each side. Here he is pictured putting the finishing touches to a new sign for the George in South Street, Bridport.

Above The much-loved cricket commentator Brian Johnston (centre) pulls a pint of Palmers in celebration of the re-opening of the Ropemakers in Bridport in 1989.

The Brewing Process

The finest British malted barley is stored on the top floor of the brewhouse.

The correct combination of barleys that form the grist for the particular beer to be brewed is then tipped into the hopper (above), which feeds the screening machine on the floor below (left).

This machine was installed in 1885 and, though now powered by electricity, can still be powered by the brewery's waterwheel. From here the malted barley passes down to the mill on the floor below. From the mill a bucket conveyor takes it to the grist case on the top floor, where it is stored until the following morning when the brewing process begins.

The grist (milled malted barley) is mashed with hot spring liquor (water) and the mash then enters the mash turn (right).

The mash is then sparged by hot liquor, this process produces the malt extract (above).

The taps are then set (right) and the malt extract then enters the underback on the floor below.

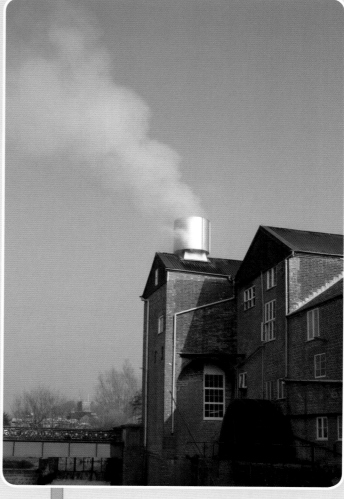

When the malt extract enters the copper it is known as wort. It used to be boiled by a coal furnace behind this door (top left). This process was stopped in 1973 as it was difficult to control. Today an external boiler boils the wort.

Palmers always brew with the finest British whole leaf hops (above left).

Hops are added to the wort in the copper (left). They are added to ale in order to impart aroma, flavour and bitterness, and they also act as a natural preservative.

Head Brewer, Darren Batten, takes a sample from the copper.

The ale is then cooled and enters one of the fermenting vessels in the Tun Room (left). Many of these vessels date back to the early part of the twentieth century.

Palmers yeast is then added to the brew and the seven-day fermentation process begins (below left).

Two days after the brew enters the fermenting vessel the yeast is skimmed into a yeast wagon below (below).

After seven days of fermentation, the ale is racked into casks and matured in the beer cellar for a few days (above).

One cask from every brew is taken to the sample room, so that it can be tasted and checked during its natural lifespan (right).

Palmers draymen, who are responsible for all the brewery's deliveries, have an excellent reputation for their politeness, helpfulness and efficiency (below).

Another of John Palmer's projects came to fruition on 21 November 1985. The company had been out of the retail business of selling beers, wines and spirits to the general public for over ten years and so it was a great moment when Palmers Wine Store was opened. The store was described by Colin Parnell of *Decanter* magazine who officially opened it as 'an architectural gem of brick and pine'. Harold Puley, who had overseen much of the brewery's surveying work for several decades, designed the store to much acclaim, though sadly within two years he had died at a comparatively young age. The store continues to thrive under the management of Mark Banham and now hosts over 800 wines from all around the world.

In a rural area such as West Dorset the decline of farming and agriculture hit hard. In Bridport, the traditional textile industries, particularly the production of rope and twine, died out altogether. To compensate for this the tourism industry became increasingly important and was given a noticeable lift by the naming of the historic seashore as the 'Jurassic Coast' and its selection as a World Heritage Site in 2001. The disappearance of traditional old-fashioned farms meant that a number of old houses became retirement or country homes for the relatively affluent, many of whom still worked in London or elsewhere and used their Dorset houses only at the weekends or during holidays. Palmers adapted to these changes with imagination and flexibility. Tourism has also been boosted in recent years by the filming of a number of TV series in the locality. *Harbour Lights*, which starred Nick Berry, was shot in West Bay, while *River Cottage* put its presenter Hugh Fearnley-Whittingstall and West Dorset firmly on the tourist trail.

Throughout this period the business has been under the stewardship of a new generation of Palmers, John and Cleeves. The elder brother John is Managing Director and Cleeves is Sales and Marketing Director. They have made an effective combination and they are determined to pass on the family business in even better health to the next generation. John married Lucille Jarrold in April 1989 and Cleeves married Edwina de Candamo in December 1994. John and Lucille have four daughters and Cleeves and Edwina have a daughter and a son. Both are quintessentially Dorset men, both brothers live in West Dorset, send their children to Dorset schools and support Dorset institutions. In the period in which they have been in charge of Palmers the image of beer and of public houses has changed quite dramatically and Palmers has kept pace with this change.

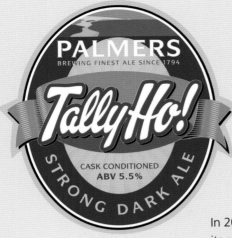

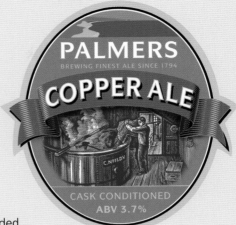

In 2008, Palmers re-branded
its range of ales, producing
a set of pump clips featuring
newly designed liveries.

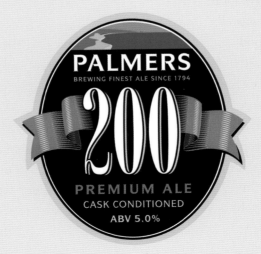

Today, Palmers produce a wide range of beers. Tally Ho! is a 'strong dark ale', first born in 1949 and named after a quite different beer from the Adnams stable in East Anglia, weighs in at 5.5 per cent Alcohol by Volume. (ABV had replaced the old, and slightly obscure method of defining alcoholic strength by 'specific gravity' in 1990s.) This continues to be a real beer-drinker's beer, a real ale par excellence with a dark, nutty taste and a cult following.

At the other end of the strength scale comes Copper Ale, which at only 3.7 per cent ABV is the sort of beer you can drink in the middle of the day without falling asleep. It now accounts for nearly 30 per cent of the company's ale sales. In between comes Palmers Best Bitter (aka India Pale Ale) at 4.2 per cent ABV; Dorset Gold at 4.5 per cent ABV which is golden and slightly fuller; and Palmers 200 Premium Ale at a hefty 5.0 per cent ABV, once described by the beer guru Roger Protz as 'complex, a finely balanced blend of malt, hops and quenching citric fruitiness from the yeast'. All five are brewed at the Old Brewery, which still remains at the heart of the family business. Like the company itself the brewery is an interesting blend of ancient and modern, full of memories of the past but also of plans for the future. Most importantly, of course, it is a source of regular and plentiful everyday beer. If you want to see for yourself you can take a two-hour tour of the brewery from Easter until the end of September and sample a glass or two of the product. Tickets are available from the spacious modern Palmers Wine Store, which still offers everything from Palmers own Golden Cap whisky to arcane vintages of fine wines from all over the world.

In February 1997 Ray Major, who had been a member of staff at the brewery for over 50 years, retired at the age of 72. During his last week of employment, he unveiled a plaque commemorating the 100th anniversary of the Palmer family's ownership of the brewery. Ray had joined the brewery after wartime service with the Royal Navy. He had been trained as a painter and decorator but he eventually became a 'jack of all trades', slotting into many different roles within the production and packaging teams. Sadly he died after too short a retirement in 2003 at the age of 78.

There are now 57 pubs in the Palmers estate. Many of them are in Dorset although there are now 15 in Devon and Somerset. Unlike the houses of some breweries Palmers pubs are quite deliberately unostentatious in their branding.

Charity Begins at Home

Palmers Brewery has always played its part in maintaining the close links between the brewing industry and charitable institutions, making substantial donations in money and in kind to a number of local beneficiaries as a way of thanking the community for its continued support.

In the early 1970s the brewery gave the land that sites the Bridport branch of the St John Ambulance. The Bridport Leisure Centre is on a peppercorn rent from the brewery. The centre was originally funded by the sale of land gifted by Palmers to the West Dorset Sports Trust that runs it. Funds from the sale were bolstered by public sector money, raising sufficient capital for its initial development.

Palmers have also given a significant amount of money through the years to both the Joseph Weld Hospice Trust and CancerCare Dorset, which have now merged and are known as the Weldmar Hospicecare Trust. More recently the charities assisted by the brewery have included the Chesil Trust, a Dorset based charity that helps young or less able bodied people to sail in the world famous waters of Weymouth and Portland that will host the Olympic regatta in 2012, the Dorset & Somerset Air Ambulance Trust and the RNLI, of which Tony Palmer was President of the Bridport branch from the mid-1970s until 1986 when he died.

All that distinguishes them, apart from the excellence of their food and drink and the friendliness and efficiency of their staff, is the trademark Palmers blue paint, which embellishes their facades, their inn signs and their delivery lorries.

Many of these houses are old favourites with a long history of Palmers ownership. The Pilot Boat in Lyme Regis is still doing good business; the Three Horseshoes at Burton Bradstock; the Crown at Puncknowle, the Marquis of Lorne at Nettlecombe, the White Horse at Litton Cheney and many more besides. Over the county border you could sip a pint of Tally Ho! at the Who'd A Thought it in Glastonbury or the Watermans Arms at Ashprington near Totnes as well as at another nine pubs in Somerset and four in Devon. You'd need to have your wits about you to realise that you were in a Palmers house though you should rest assured that each pub serves first-class beer, has an original menu and a offers a generous array of wines from around the world.

Palmers Staff

The Palmers Brewery staff, summer 2008.

Back row (left to right) Anthony Trevett,
Chris Hoskins, Nick Tuck, Colin Northover,
Luke Machin, David Whittingham,
Andrew Samways.

Third row Tim Joy, Steve Clark, Peter Bustin,
John Short, Rob Walkey, Jim Traquair,
John Abbott, Barry Knight, Mike Ramsden.

Second row Jason Hawker, David Bennett,
Kevin Haines, Paul Smith, Neil Wheeler,
Dean Sweet, Graham Symes, Roger Dixon,
Ed Mamanta, Will Good, Chris Coram,
Wayne Causley, Mark Banham.

Front row Darren Batten, Clare Pimbley,
Sarah New, Jacky Follett, Linda Hobday,
Cleeves Palmer, John Palmer, Tim Woodrow,
Jane Clark, Ronnie Mace, Tom Hutchings,
Gary Adcock.

Insets (left to right) Tony Whittingham,
Emma Eaton, John Barber, Kristine Tozer.

Staff with 20 Years Service
Past and Present

Photographed in 2008.

Back row (left to right) Anthony Trevett, Jim Traquair, *Dennis Legg*,
Burt Isaacs, Ronnie Mace, *Bill Almond*, Nick Tuck.

Front row *Eddie Cook*, Andrew Samways, Cleeves Palmer,
John Palmer, *Mike Ramsden*, Tim Woodrow.

names in italics denote staff who have retired.

John and Cleeves have a good team around them; Tim Woodrow joined the brewery as sales manager in 1985 after 13 years with Guinness. Six years later he became Palmers first technical director after making an enormous contribution in setting up supply agreements to an array of wholesalers as well as professionalising the company's offering to its tenanted estate. Before Tim's years at Guinness he had worked for Gibbs Mew, where he completed his brewing pupilage. Tim is currently the brewery's Tenanted Trade Director, and in 2007 he was joined by Tenanted Trade Manager Tom Hutchings.

Adrian Wood was appointed head brewer in 1990, only the third person to hold the post since 1945, and he carried on the same traditions as his predecessors. In 2006 Adrian left the company and Darren Batten succeeded him in September that year. Darren, another West Dorset man, had originally joined the company in 1992 after graduating with a degree in biology. In the summer of 2006 he was awarded his diploma in brewing after several years of studying and his labours were rewarded with a natural promotion.

After more than two hundred years of brewing beer in this beautiful part of the country the Old Brewery is still going strong. In time the younger members of the present Palmer family will take over from their fathers and one of Britain's most successful family businesses will pass on to a fifth generation.

It is a uniquely English institution making a uniquely English beverage and serving it up in a uniquely English situation. Palmers are proud to be Palmers and the rest of us should be proud too that such traditional family businesses still flourish and prosper. Perhaps one should drink to that – preferably by raising a pint of Palmers to our lips and expressing the hope that the last few centuries or so are simply a modest beginning.

Acknowledgements

I am extremely grateful to His Royal Highness The Earl of Wessex for so kindly writing the foreword to this book.

There have been many people involved in this book's production and grateful thanks go to them all. Richard Sims carried much of the early research out; over the space of two years he found out so much about the history of the brewery, that even John and I did not know! All his material was instrumentally important for the writer Tim Heald, who is of international renown. The editor, Julian Flanders then fine-tuned Tim's work, Carole Melbourne created the book's design and layout and skilfully photographed the many artefacts and people that feature in this publication and last but not least Nick Heal, who prepared the book for print.

Cleeves Palmer
December 2008

This photograph of three generations of the Palmer family was taken at Little Wych on the occasion of Bob and Elsie's Golden Wedding on 8 October 1964.

Standing John, Tony & Nora Palmer
Seated Susan, Bob, Cleeves, Elsie and Anne Palmer

H.M.S. EDGAR

CAPTAIN JOHN PALMER (1770 – 1828)

On H.M.S. Edgar he served as a Lieutenant 1805–06, he was promoted to Commander in 1806 and to Captain in 1814. When he died in 1828, he only left his wife and children £ 1–15s–4d. It was no wonder she felt compelled to write to the 'Compassionate Fund' for impoverished widows. She also wrote to H.M. King George IV for his help stating that: "in an interview my late husband had with His Majesty, He was pleased to say that in view of his service testimonials, His Majesty would be a friend to his children for life" King George IV's response is not known, but what is known is that all their children were well educated and that his widow was never short of money again.

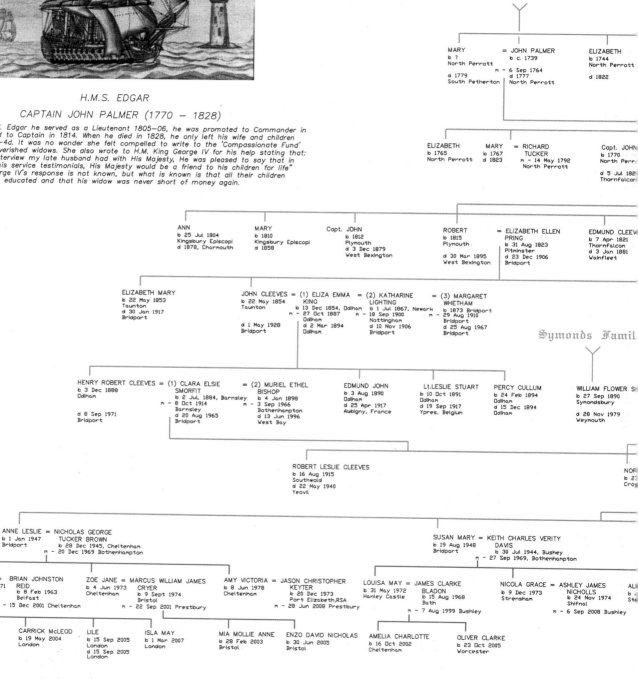

Palmer Family

MARY
b ?
North Perrott
d 1779
South Petherton

= JOHN PALMER
b c. 1739
m – 6 Sep 1764
d 1777
North Perrott

ELIZABETH
b 1744
North Perrott
d 1822

ELIZABETH
b 1765
North Perrott

MARY
b 1767
d 1823

= RICHARD
TUCKER
m – 14 May 1792
North Perrott

Capt. JOHN
b 1770
North Perr
d 5 Jul 182
Thornfalcon

ANN
b 25 Jul 1804
Kingsbury Episcopi
d 1878, Charmouth

MARY
b 1810
Kingsbury Episcopi
d 1858

Capt. JOHN
b 1812
Plymouth
d 3 Dec 1879
West Bexington

ROBERT
b 1815
Plymouth
d 30 Mar 1895
West Bexington

= ELIZABETH ELLEN
PRING
b 31 Aug 1823
Pitminster
d 23 Dec 1906
Bridport

EDMUND CLEEV
b 7 Apr 1821
Thornfalcon
d 3 Jan 1891
Wainfleet

ELIZABETH MARY
b 22 May 1853
Taunton
d 30 Jan 1917
Bridport

JOHN CLEEVES =
b 22 May 1854
Taunton
d 1 May 1928
Bridport

(1) ELIZA EMMA
KING
b 13 Dec 1854, Odiham
m – 27 Oct 1887
Odiham
d 2 Mar 1894
Odiham

= (2) KATHARINE
LIGHTING
b 1 Jul 1867, Newark
m – 18 Sep 1900
Nottingham
d 10 Nov 1906
Bridport

= (3) MARGARET
WHETHAM
b 1873 Bridport
m – 29 Aug 1910
Bridport
d 25 Aug 1967
Bridport

Symonds Famil

HENRY ROBERT CLEEVES =
b 3 Dec 1888
Odiham
d 8 Sep 1971
Bridport

(1) CLARA ELSIE
SMORFIT
b 2 Jul 1884, Barnsley
m – 8 Oct 1914
Barnsley
d 20 Aug 1965
Bridport

= (2) MURIEL ETHEL
BISHOP
b 4 Jan 1898
m – 3 Sep 1966
Bothenhampton
d 13 Jun 1996
West Bay

EDMUND JOHN
b 3 Aug 1890
Odiham
d 25 Apr 1917
Aubigny, France

Lt.LESLIE STUART
b 10 Oct 1891
Odiham
d 19 Sep 1917
Ypres, Belgium

PERCY CULLUM
b 24 Feb 1894
Odiham
d 15 Dec 1894

WILLIAM FLOWER S
b 27 Sep 1890
Symondsbury
d 28 Nov 1979
Weymouth

ROBERT LESLIE CLEEVES
b 16 Aug 1915
Southwold
d 22 May 1940
Yeovil

NOR
b 2
Croy

ANNE LESLIE = NICHOLAS GEORGE
b 1 Jan 1947   TUCKER BROWN
Bridport   b 28 Dec 1945, Cheltenham
m – 20 Dec 1969 Bothenhampton

SUSAN MARY = KEITH CHARLES VERITY
b 19 Aug 1948   DAVIS
Bridport   b 30 Jul 1944, Bushey
m – 27 Sep 1969, Bothenhampton

CLARE
b 5 Apr 1971
Cheltenham

= BRIAN JOHNSTON
REID
b 8 Feb 1963
Belfast
m – 15 Dec 2001 Cheltenham

ZOE JANE = MARCUS WILLIAM JAMES
b 4 Jun 1973   CRYER
Cheltenham   b 9 Sept 1974
Bristol
m – 22 Sep 2001 Prestbury

AMY VICTORIA = JASON CHRISTOPHER
b 8 Jun 1978   KEYTER
Cheltenham   b 20 Dec 1973
Port Elizabeth,RSA
m – 28 Jun 2008 Prestbury

LOUISA MAY = JAMES CLARKE
b 31 May 1972   BLADON
Hanley Castle   b 15 Aug 1968
Bath
m – 7 Aug 1999 Bushley

NICOLA GRACE = ASHLEY JAMES
b 9 Dec 1973   NICHOLLS
Strensham   b 24 Nov 1974
Shifnal
m – 6 Sep 2008 Bushley

ALI
b
Str

AOIFE GRACE
b 26 Sep 2002
New York

CARRICK McLEOD
b 19 May 2004
London

LILE
b 15 Sep 2005
London
d 15 Sep 2005
London

ISLA MAY
b 1 Mar 2007
London

MIA MOLLIE ANNE
b 28 Feb 2003
Bristol

ENZO DAVID NICHOLAS
b 30 Jun 2005
Bristol

AMELIA CHARLOTTE
b 16 Oct 2002
Cheltenham

OLIVER CLARKE
b 23 Oct 2005
Worcester